THE *Bluffer's*

JAZZ

Paul Barnes and Peter Gammond

Colette House
52-55 Piccadilly
London W1J 0DX
United Kingdom

Email: info@bluffers.com
Website: bluffers.com
Twitter: @BluffersGuide

First published 1987
This edition published 2013
Copyright © Bluffer's® 2013

Publisher: Thomas Drewry
Publishing Director: Brooke McDonald

Series Editor: David Allsop
Design and Illustration: Jim Shannon

With acknowledgements to the late Peter Clayton,
co-author of the original edition.
Additional contributions by John Lewis.

All rights reserved. No part of this publication
may be reproduced, stored in a retrieval system
or transmitted in any form or by any means, electronic,
mechanical, photocopying, recording or otherwise,
without the prior permission of Bluffer's®.

A CIP Catalogue record for this book
is available from the British Library.

Bluffer's Guide®, Bluffer's® and Bluff Your Way®
are registered trademarks.

ISBN: 978-1-909365-44-5 (print)
       978-1-909365-45-2 (ePub)
       978-1-909365-46-9 (Kindle)

CONTENTS

If you've always assumed that Ruby Braff was a female wrestler and Randy Brecker is a kind of aphrodisiac muesli, don't be put off.

ALL THAT JAZZ

Jazz is a good subject for bluffing because whoever happens to contradict you is almost certainly bluffing as well. This is because no one seems to know for certain how, where or why it all began. So your theories should, in theory, be as good as anyone else's. You may also hold the most outrageous critical opinions (for example, that Bunk Johnson was a fluent and inventive trumpet player, or that Jelly Roll Morton was a model of modesty and self-effacement), and citizens of the jazz world, far from regarding you as a nutter, will declare respect for your viewpoint and earnestly discuss the basis of your contentions.

However, there are three notes of caution. The earnest jazz enthusiast is as earnest as anyone you are ever likely to meet, so:

1. Never make jokes about jazz. If you do, make them with a fairly straight face or, at most, a slightly apologetic smile.

2. Whatever line you take, stick to it – no matter where it might lead you.

3. Don't agree with anyone completely. You might generously concur now and then in moderate mutual admiration of the art of Dink Johnson (or whoever is in the frame), but make sure that it is for different reasons. Total agreement will only lead to a reputation for indifference and might even raise suspicion.

One advantage of jazz over other kinds of music is that you don't have to listen to it if you don't want to. And plenty of people who do listen to it don't actually listen either, because they have their own agenda. While the music is being played, live or on record, they are arguing, very loudly, about how – or even if – the contents of rare and crackling old 78s and battered LPs should be transferred to CD. They are questioning whether this or that presenter/editor/columnist/authority knows what he or she is talking about.

They are pontificating on matters such as exactly when Louis Armstrong stopped being great, why Miles Davis was the way he was, what Anthony Braxton's geometric titles really mean, and why it can't be jazz without a banjo. They are asking whoever is sitting next to them which two Blue Note sleeves were designed by Andy Warhol, and whether David Stone Martin's sleeves were often better than the music within them.

This chatter used to die down only during a bass solo when it was suddenly apparent that everything had gone comparatively quiet. But then bass players realised that the subtlety and brilliance of their playing was being masked by the sound of other instruments, so they fought back by purchasing amplifiers of their own and winding up the wick to suit themselves. Any chatter during a drum solo is usually pointless as it is too noisy even to hear your own bickering.

Do feel free to join in all this innocent fun. After all, there is no reason not to, and it's one way to advance your own credentials. If you've always assumed that Ruby Braff was a female wrestler and Randy Brecker is a kind of aphrodisiac muesli, don't be put off. Ignorance has never deterred others, and in this kind of verbal skirmishing, he who hesitates is defeated. So, get in there and grab your share of pontification.

This short but definitive guide sets out to conduct you through the main danger zones encountered in jazz discussions, and to equip you with a vocabulary and an evasive technique that will minimise the risk of being rumbled as a bluffer. It will give you a few easy-to-learn hints and techniques designed to allow you to be accepted as a jazz aficionado of rare ability and experience. But it will do more. It will give provide you with the tools to impress legions of marvelling listeners with your knowledge and insight – without anyone discovering that before reading it you didn't know the difference between a trumpophone and a mobile phone.

If you feel like suggesting that
the word 'jazz' is derived from
the African-American word 'jizz',
meaning a certain horizontal exercise,
then there's nothing to stop you.

BACK TO THE ROOTS

The glorious thing about jazz is that there is neither a universally accepted definition of the word nor a factually provable account of the music's origins.

You might want to maintain, for instance, that the word 'jazz' is simply a corruption of 'jars', arising from the fact that an improvised, percussive sort of music was first played by the people of what became The Gambia. They used glass jars, washed ashore in 1756 after a consignment of Frank Cooper's Oxford marmalade went down off West Africa, striking them with dried vulture bones. Always be specific about stuff like this; it adds conviction, and such detailed knowledge should deter contradiction. Even if it's patent nonsense.

Or if you feel like suggesting that the word 'jazz' is derived from the African-American word 'jizz', meaning a certain horizontal exercise, then there's nothing to stop you. Unless you happen to be talking to the likes of jazz historians such as Paul Oliver, Alyn Shipton or Scott Yanow, who will likely have embarked on some even more abstruse theory before you can get a word in.

You could point out that more recent research has revealed that, contrary to popular belief, jazz really began in 1846 when a famous Belgian called Adolphe Sax invented the saxophone. For years Sax was the only famous Belgian. He originally had the military and circus band market in mind, but there was a decidedly hepcat (*see* 'Glossary') element in his make-up. Contemporary accounts claimed that when he was developing the instrument, blowing experimental licks in his workshop, he sounded like an amalgam of Lester Young, Charlie Parker, Sidney Bechet, Gerry Mulligan, Paul Desmond and, er, others. Sadly, this is mere hearsay – not helped by the fact that none of these noted jazz musicians had yet been born.

Ironically, early practitioners of so-called classic jazz repudiated the saxophone, probably because they suspected that in years to come certain critics would make menacing noises about the purity of the music being sullied by its blaringly intrusive sound.

You could easily quote an example of this prophecy being fulfilled when fundamentalist post-war British jazz critic Rex Harris wrote sniffily: 'The tenor-saxophonist Coleman Hawkins possessed great powers of improvisation which, had they been canalised into a different medium of expression, e.g., the clarinet, might well have secured him a permanent place in jazz.' (*Jazz*, Pelican Books, 1952.) When 'The Hawk' came across this, he was said to have been deeply affected, declaring: 'Oh, my goodness gracious, if I'd had the faintest inkling of this, I'd have taken better care of the old liquorice stick.' Or words to that effect.

Then there is the music itself. You might perhaps have wondered about all those interminable bass and drum solos. Long ago, bass players and drummers established inalienable rights to self-indulgent solo displays, often of inordinate length and tediousness. This is mainly because, given the bulky nature of the tools of their trade, only the bass player and the drummer were likely to possess their own transport. Their ownership of cars meant that when it came to getting a lift home other members of the band were beholden to them. Thus did fear of being stranded come to outweigh artistic scruples. (A notable exception to this general principle was one-time Humphrey Lyttelton bassist, Brian Brocklehurst, who cheerfully pedalled from gig to gig carrying the big fiddle on his bike.)

♔

> Long ago, bass players and drummers established inalienable rights to self-indulgent solo displays, often of inordinate length and tediousness.

Be very wary of bluffing with genuine jazz musicians. They aren't likely to be bothered with the Gambian theory of the origins of jazz or Sax's experimental riffing. Apart from the union rate for the job, their main preoccupation is with the chord sequences. One horn blower, reputed to be 'Slusher' Treadwell, not only knew every chord of every tune in the band's repertoire but also had the knack of enunciating some of them while actually playing his instrument. This is no mean accomplishment. Hold an egg cup so that its bowl covers your lips and try saying clearly, out of the side of your mouth, 'Don't forget the G seventh.'

JAZZ TYPES

There are really only three kinds of jazz that you need to know about:

1. **Traditional** Jazz conceived and recorded before 1940; mostly a collective improvisation based loosely on 'When the Saints Go Marching In'.

2. **Modern** Jazz conceived and recorded since 1940.

It is not actually possible, though many critics try to do it, to like or support both Trad and Mod. It is akin to saying that you support both the Conservative and Labour parties at the same time. So decide which you uphold and decry the other on every occasion; or, if you can't make up your mind what you like, stroke your chin and judiciously say you prefer:

3. **Mainstream** Jazz of a sort of Lib-Dem persuasion, or 'middle of the road'. The term was conjured up one restless night by the eminent critic Stanley Dance after an evening at a jam session involving Duke Ellington and members of his band, together with Brad Gowans, Horsecollar Draper and Eddie Condon. Lost for a word

to describe what he heard he sought to dignify the proceedings by calling it 'mainstream'.

JAZZ HISTORY

Compared with institutions such as pawnbroking and opera, jazz is too young to have much history, which hasn't stopped it accumulating a quite disproportionate body of myth, fable and legend. If it were not for a few solid and unassailable truths like Fats Waller, Pinetop Smith's death certificate, Ronnie Scott's club and Thelonious Monk's version of 'Nice Work If You Can Get it', one might suspect that the jazz press had made the whole thing up. The truth is, only 75% of it was made up, chiefly by Jelly Roll Morton (1890-1941), with a few inept contributions from Bunk Johnson and sundry mendacious jazzmen.

A myth of Morton's making that could have been very helpful was his declaration that he personally invented jazz in 1902. Even his business card modestly proclaimed him as 'Inventor of Jazz and Stomps'. If the so-called experts had had the sense to go along with his claim, jazz would have a concise, tidy history and we should be free to concentrate on listening to the music instead of arguing about it. Jazz history books would have been able to divide events neatly into AM and PM – ante-Morton and post-Morton.

Always remember: the fabric of the history of jazz is liberally embroidered with names, a roll call from Irving Aaronson to Mike Zwerin. Never heard of them? Don't worry; your audience is unlikely to have done, either. In between, just to keep it interesting and to make it harder for newcomers to crack the code, are numerous other characters, many of whom probably didn't exist at all. You might like to keep in conversational reserve a reference to Stavin' Chain, a genuine jazz-sounding name so marginal as to be practically off the page. Elsewhere we offer a fine bargain selection of names such as Nesuhi Ertegun, Eustern Woodfork, Husk O'Hare, Ishman Bracey, Hociel Tebo, Porridge Foot Pete, Deaf Rhubarb Blenkinsop, John Fallstitch, Wim Poppink and Cornelius Plumb. You are perfectly entitled to disbelieve any or all of these, but you have to admit they have tremendous potential to lend colour to a conversation. And, believe it or not, some of them have actually figured in some quite respectable CD inlays.

The name that is totally unavoidable in jazz history is good old **Jelly Roll Morton,** about whom it is imperative to know a handful of basic facts – such as that he was a pimp, a gambler, a pool shark and a small-time hustler involved in lots of dubious enterprises; he also had a diamond set into one of his front teeth. His given first name was Ferdinand (and his original surname was Lamothe or Le Menthe, which he changed to Morton because he didn't like being called 'Frenchy'). He acquired the nickname 'Jelly Roll' which, like 90% of all names and words used in jazz, has more to do with sexual prowess than musical ability. The common belief is that Morton must have been rather good at it, but not according to his widow, who recalled, somewhere or other, that he was rather less than outstanding in this department.

Once you've absorbed all of this vital information,

you need to store a few trifles, e.g., that he was one of the first musicians to compose pieces specifically for jazz performance; that he was a superb, if occasionally prim-sounding, piano player and a very skilled bandleader; and that while he irritated people with his boasting, he irritated them even more by proving that much of what he bragged about was true. Moreover, he did it all (hear him on those famous interviews with Alan Lomax) with the avuncular charm of a real Southern gentleman.

Morton was born in New Orleans and consistently lied about his age, perversely claiming to be older than he really was. He let people assume he had been born in 1885, and it wasn't until 1985 when his 100th anniversary celebrations were in full swing that fresh research suggested that his true birthdate was 1890.

Bunk Johnson was another who was economical with the truth concerning his real age, insisting he was born earlier than he was. What helped him with this fiction was that he actually looked old, even as a young man. He persuaded a few eager pioneer historians to believe him, and the record is being set straight only now by learned gentlemen at various US universities.

You can likely now see why it doesn't really matter if you occasionally throw in a few dubious nuggets masquerading as facts. Jazz history totters on the shaky ground of misinformation. Nevertheless, it is always a good thing to have a few firm facts handy, and one we know for certain is that the first jazz recording was made in 1917 by the Original Dixieland Jazz Band (*see* 'Horn Blowers').

UP THE RIVER AND ALL THAT JAZZ

Jazz, according to one popular and largely unverifiable theory, was invented in New Orleans around 1am on 17 November 1887, the creation of a Creole barber's assistant called **Thermidus Brown,** known to acquaintances and admirers alike as 'Jazz-bo' on account of his being such a snappy dresser. He was tootling on a battered cornet, bought in 1867 from an ex-Civil War bandsman called Ephraim Draper. As always, by 1am he had succumbed to the influence of local rye whisky and began to mistime his phrases, giving the tune a strangely propulsive sort of quality. This greatly excited the customers in 'Loopy' Dumaine's lakeside crawfish restaurant where he was playing at the time. Later authorities came to define what he was doing as syncopation, but to Thermidus it was simply an inner memory of the banjo rhythms from the old plantation where he served his time as a slave in his younger days. This might be plausible had he been sober enough to remember anything.

We don't know much about Thermidus, except that his father was a mule-breaker called Brown and that he was born in New Orleans circa 1847. On 5 July 1894 he was aboard a riverboat en route for St Louis, where he was apparently going to invent ragtime. But at 2am, drunk, of course, he fell overboard and drowned.

You can afford to look sorrowful if recounting this story and, if you feel bold enough, you might even start humming 'Ol' Man River'. And if you really want to push your luck, sing:

He mus' know sumpin'
But don't say nuthin'...

...which might be good advice for you.

Despite Thermidus's tragic demise, local dance-band musicians had picked up the exciting new sounds that he'd created and by 1897 or so they were to be heard everywhere in New Orleans. One player worth noting was the ex-editor of a scandal sheet known as *The Cricket* (rare copies of which now sell for thousands of dollars). This renegade journalist-turned-jazzman was one **Charles 'Buddy' Bolden.**

Buddy's main – indeed his only – claim to fame was the loudness of his playing – it being said, with the straightest of faces, that he could be heard '14 miles away on a clear night'. As nobody who was 14 miles away at the time has ever come forward to verify this, it is yet another jazz legend that has to be treated with a modicum of suspicion. Proclaim it anyway if the subject of loudness comes up.

The would-be jazz bluffer may already sense the deep and treacherous currents of moonshine that ebb and flow beneath the surface of jazz history. The options are to express an unshakeable belief in these legends (a standpoint taken by many writers of jazz books); or to condemn them as being obviously ridiculous (as difficult an argument to uphold as trying to maintain that Noah never built an ark).

The next thing that happened to jazz was that it went 'up the river'. This is a useful phrase to bandy about and will ensure nods of knowing approval from anyone who has heard it and not had a clue what it meant. It is nonetheless a vital moment in the evolution of jazz and so you must pretend to be *au fait* with the circumstances surrounding it. Again, only the faintest vestiges of the truth have been hinted at here. The fact is that an unscrupulous individual with the doom-laden name of Fate Marable, who had come from Paducah, Kentucky, and was a third-rate exponent of the steam calliope (an inefficient instrument which suffered – as you can see in old silent films – from leaky valves), began to feel that New Orleans was getting overcrowded with jazz musicians. Especially the good ones like Louis Armstrong. So, for a modest sum, he bought himself the right to act as a sort of employment agent for hiring jazz musicians to play on riverboats that plied up and down the Mississippi.

He paid them enough to tempt them to make the journey upstream to far-flung places like St Louis, knowing that they would never be able to afford to get back. Which left things much better for his clients in New Orleans. He would lure the unsuspecting riverboat mugs with posters that made Chicago look like a bracing seaside town and off they would go, hoping to find fame and fortune, with a one-way ticket in one hand and an instrument case in the other. None of them knew that, back home in Paducah, he had once run a travel agency.

EARLY INFLUENCES

RAGTIME

The theory of the dawn of ragtime was first proposed by Theolosiphus J Elfleikmann Jr II in 'Ragtime Re-Defined: a Collection of Papers Read at the University of Milneburg, July 7–15, 1943'. He asserted that ragtime was first invented in Fred's Eating House on West 37th Street, St Louis, because the pianist had hiccups. This assertion is deeply unreliable but feel free to make it nonetheless – even if you can't remember Elfleikmann's name. Few people, jazz enthusiasts or not, would have the nerve to contradict you. It could be a bluff, but few would dare call it (and haven't since the first edition of this book was published over 25 years ago).

All you need to know about ragtime is that it began as dance music in the red-light districts of African-American communities – principally in St Louis and New Orleans. Its main characteristic, other than being played on the piano, is that it is 'syncopated'. Syncopation is a very useful word to remember when discussing jazz influences – or, indeed, any musical genre which often sounds out of tune.

The truth is that ragtime most likely originated from

the use of a piano with several missing keys. There were plenty around in speakeasies at the time – second-hand, ex-gold-rush stock, many of them badly shot up.

In any discussion about ragtime it is possible, and possibly advisable, to adopt a particularly purist standpoint. It is the one jazz-oriented subject that the general musical conversationalist is likely to veer toward on the strength of having seen a film called *The Sting*. This brought the name of **Scott Joplin,** ragtime's most famous exponent, very much to the front of the music bluffer's repertoire.

Joplin (1868-1917) has become almost contemptibly familiar. Any attempts to bandy his name about as the only one that really matters in ragtime should immediately be rebuffed by dark suggestions that James Scott, Arthur Marshall, Joe Jordan, Eubie Blake and so on were actually superior. Untrue but tenable – and few will have done the necessary groundwork to be able to argue.

Joplin established a few of the unshakeable tenets of ragtime, like 'Notice! Don't play this piece fast. It is never right to play "ragtime" fast. Author.' It was a sort of government health warning that he had printed on many of his pieces. Perversely, he made his name with a work called 'Maple Leaf Rag' which he, and a whole lot of others, always played at a high rate of knots.

Scott Joplin was a very ambitious fellow and became fixated on the idea of writing a ragtime opera which he called *Treemonisha*. He sank all his well-earned royalties into it, and personally financed a performance in Harlem.

But it went no further and its failure drove him to insanity.

He enjoyed considerable posthumous success, though, which was no good to him at all. Had he lived as long as the ragtime lyricist, composer and pianist Eubie Blake, he might have seen the day when *Treemonisha* was put on in a respectable opera house. But he would doubtless have been more interested in the fact that the rest of his music began to make big money (for other people) in the shape of film scores, ballets and commercial jingles. Incidentally, when Eubie Blake eventually died in his late 90s in 1983, he was reported as saying: 'If I'd known I was going to live this long I'd have taken better care of myself.' (He was a noted heavy smoker and drinker.)

Whatever you do, resist the temptation to attempt an impression of 'The Entertainer', the theme of *The Sting* (and probably Joplin's best-known work); it will be extremely irritating for everyone concerned. Simply point out that, unlike most jazz, ragtime actually exists in written scores and, for some, these have become the Gospel According to St Joshua (as Joshua Rifkin is known by ragtime aficionados).

Rifkin, as you must affect to know, was a well turned-out, decently groomed American musicologist, a specialist in medieval music and sometime jug-blower, who had the bright idea of playing and recording Joplin straight. Unfortunately, this made ragtime accessible to anybody. The ragtime specialist will therefore find it politic to cast aspersions on Rifkin's so-called decency and purity. Genuine ragtime purveyors would not have sounded (or even looked) quite so respectable. Apart from the fact that they would have been playing a knackered old joanna rather than a Steinway, would not have been wearing tails and might even have smiled, they would probably have been well refreshed with whatever was going free in the alcohol line. Mustering such evidence, what you should add, with some authority, is that they would have played in a much less inhibited style.

Another good name to throw into the ring is Max Morath (who generally wore a bowler hat – often a sign of unimpeachable authenticity), pointing out that his way of playing is probably nearer to the 'jig' style of a well-known ragtime composer called Tom Turpin. A handful of names like these can easily be culled from books like *Ragtime Rarities*, edited by the unusually named Trebor Jay Tichenor.

You might make a start with Harvey M Babcock, Mattie Harl Burgess, E Warren Furry, J Bodewalt Lampe, Julia Lee Niebergall or Frank X McFadden. Jot them down somewhere. Most of these, casually trotted out, could easily take the wind out of the sails of even an established, thunderously boring ragtime know-it-all.

You will have to gauge very carefully the strength of the conversational competition but, if you think you can do it without getting caught, by all means hint that you know quite a bit about a certain **Louis Moreau Gottschalk** (1829-1869). Born in New Orleans, he became a virtuoso pianist – people compared him with Liszt – and a prolific composer, and some of his works based on Louisiana folk dances do have an extraordinary ragtime-like flavour. If you feel like being really contentious, you might try arguing that he was the true begetter of ragtime.

THE BLUES

The blues are such an intrinsic element of jazz that you really don't have to say much about them – not that there is that much to say about them anyway, musicologically speaking. They all have the same tune and the same chord sequence, and are all played at the same speed. Any words, when sung, are more or less the same – along the lines of:

Woke up dis mornin', a chicken walked over my face;
Woke up dis mornin', a chicken walked over my face.
Now my Baby's done gone and left me;
An' I'm startin' to hate this place.

As sung by the very best blues singers, the words are freely shouted or incanted in a rough tone, becoming less and less decipherable as verse succeeds verse. This helps to create work for scholarly commentators who feel that they merit analysis.

To be considered an authority on the blues you should claim to have spoken at least once to a British blues expert called Paul Oliver (even if it was only to say 'Hello' or 'Excuse me, that's my pint'). He is the author of most of the books that have been written on the blues and did research not only in the Deep South of the USA but in Africa, too.

If you aim to set yourself up as a real blues expert, you should not be discussing anybody who was actually commercially successful in this field (for example, Bessie Smith, so-called Empress of the Blues, or even Ma Rainey) or who frequently recorded with jazz musicians. If you once had a liking for Josh White, just don't mention it. Real blues singers, the naturally incoherent ones, all have names like Blind Willie, Deaf Tom, One-Armed Alex or Luther Rainshine. In fact you'll be on sound bluffing territory if you feel like inventing a spurious leading figure in the genre: just preface any name with the adjective 'Blind', 'Deaf' or 'Lame'. Best not to try 'Dumb', because presumably they wouldn't have enjoyed much commercial success as a singer.

A few of the better-known genuine singers who warbled in an authentically incomprehensible way, like Blind Lemon Jefferson or Lead Belly, are also perfectly acceptable. The ideal blues singer is physically and vocally handicapped and will, at most, have recorded one item called 'Black-hearted Blues No 5' which was on the obscure and unobtainable Krapp label, the only copy of which has see-through grooves and is owned by a reclusive collector in Bournemouth. His tombstone, should he ever have one, might be inscribed with the legend:

Didn't wake up dis mornin',

or perhaps

Dis is de grave of Two-Note Jake
Who, dis morning, failed to wake.

Credit for inventing the blues was claimed by a black Memphis bandmaster called WC Handy, but this has long been disregarded. At most, he gets credit for the neat idea of always having tunes that are 12 bars long, so that anyone can tell they are blues, and for the twice-repeated 'Woke up with a walkin' chicken' trademark.

Anyone looking for a clear definition, even in the most scholarly books, will be told that blues are fundamentally a state of mind. The spirit of the blues inhabits all true jazz. It's what makes it 'funky'.

> Real blues singers, the naturally incoherent ones, all have names like Blind Willie, Deaf Tom, One-Armed Alex or Luther Rainshine.

BOOGIE-WOOGIE

Boogie-woogie is essentially the blues translated as piano music. It goes under various descriptions, such as barrelhouse, honky-tonk, etc. – all labels that are redolent of lower-class origins and dissolute sexual behaviour. The scholarly interpreter of jazz (generally a blameless soul addicted to nothing more sinister than sandals, a duffel coat and a glass of shandy) often finds it an embarrassment that nearly all the basic jazz jargon derives from sexual activity.

'Boogie', as many decent souls will acknowledge with a shudder, is a Southern name for a prostitute; and 'boogie-woogie' was the secondary stage of syphilis. Hence much of the boogie-woogie that became fashionable in the 1930s bore nudge-nudge, wink-wink, sexually related titles like 'Beat me, Daddy', 'Eight to the Bar' or 'Honky-Tonk Train Blues'.

Boogie-woogie – basically 12-bar variations over a regular figured bass – ranges from the sparse tinklings of bluesy (almost melodic) Jimmy Yancey to the pounding ebullience of Pete Johnson and Albert Ammons, who must have got through two pianos a week. It inspired similar thunderous swing-band versions (that got through two loudspeakers a week) and became a basic ingredient of that early manifestation of pop known as 'rock 'n' roll'.

SWING

It is now generally accepted that the word 'swing' came into jazz from the world of sex, drugs and hamburgers.

A little-known backing singer, Delia 'Sugar' Brown, who might have been the first woman to cry out 'Oh, swing it!' to her man, was not actually referring to the music, though the fact that he was dancing at the time, wearing nothing but a complacent smile, may have helped lend ambiguity to the connection. In south-west Alabama, those who could 'swing it' were generally reckoned to be physically well-endowed in one way or another. The term gradually came to be applied to the kind of music that was inclined to set things in motion, and eventually to a kind of big-band jazz that laid particular emphasis on a propulsive beat.

Composer and big-band leader **Duke Ellington** is considered to have put swing on the map in 1931 when he wrote a controversial little number called 'It Don't Mean a Thing (If it Ain't Got That Swing)'. This tended rather to upset those folk who had got along very well without 'it' for several decades. Indeed, many thought that the coming of swing heralded the end of genuine jazz. The name went on to be taken up by biggish bands who wanted a word to describe what they were doing, apart from providing the background for dancing and making money. Swing bands were much looked down on by early jazz enthusiasts, but with the passing of the years they have now become acceptable. **Benny Goodman** was crowned 'King of Swing' by his agent (who was on 25%) and was the first jazzman to attract huge adolescent crowds, later referred to as 'bobby-soxers'. Swing itself, having allegedly been buried around 1946, became respectable and collectable in pirated recordings taken from the radio and downloaded from the internet.

The decrepit state of their instruments and the decrepit state of the players, who all drank heavily or smoked marijuana, tended to give genuine New Orleans jazz the flavour of fried boots.

WHERE THE ROOTS FLOURISHED

While New Orleans was arguably the birthplace of jazz, America's home-grown musical genre grew up in different cities around the USA. These became known as the 'cradles of jazz', and any self-respecting bluffer should be able to drone on authoritatively about the most important.

NEW ORLEANS JAZZ

Indulging a taste for New Orleans jazz is the equivalent of liking (in the classical field) the sound of crumhorns, rebecs and lutes or (in literature) of enjoying *Beowulf*. It is always a good thing in any contentious area of discussions like jazz to be an avowed purist. The purest of all purists in the jazz field is the staunch supporter of New Orleans jazz, maintaining that it is the only righteous way forward. In view of the obvious improvements in musical technique that have occurred since, it is not an easy position to sustain. However, the basic tenets are as follows (if you can be bothered to commit them to memory):

1. Everything should be played in B flat (a brief excursion now and then into F or E flat is permissible, but should not be overdone).

2. Everything should be played in an undeviating 2/4 (accenting beats 2 and 4, rather than 1 and 3).

3. There should be only one of each instrument. These are cornet, clarinet and trombone, hereafter known as the front line; and banjo, tuba and drums, hereafter known as the rhythm section. A piano is allowable, provided that it is hard of tone and seldom entirely in tune. NB: the cornet is mandatory and should be battered and slightly green (trumpets are forbidden). That is the first unbreakable law, the second and third being that it must be a banjo and not a guitar, a tuba and not a string bass.

New Orleans bands spent half their time performing in low dives where the pianos matured nicely on a diet of spilled alcohol, peanut shells and the pungent fumes of exotic substances smouldering; the other half saw them marching and making music for mourners at funerals. Going to the graveyard they played, as was only right, slow and solemn tunes. On the return trip they played fast so as not to waste any time in getting to the drinks and eats.

The decrepit state of their instruments and the decrepit state of the players, who all drank heavily or smoked marijuana, tended to give genuine New Orleans jazz the flavour of fried boots. Its general decrepitude was perhaps exaggerated in the 1940s when there was a revival of interest in the real thing, and ancient musicians, often minus such desirable assets as teeth and memories, were provided with specially battered instruments, sparking off a fanatical interest in the trad sound.

♛

New Orleans bands spent half their time marching and making music for mourners at funerals.

Anybody unaware of the aforementioned requirements for the making of New Orleans jazz might well have taken the records they bought of such revival bands back to the shop thinking there was something technically wrong with them. The connoisseur would, on the other hand, have revelled in the cracked notes, savoured the rare ability to play just off key (difficult to do deliberately), and admired the elephantine rhythm with the unique flavour that comes from the intermingling of plinked banjo and plonked bass.

Once the original New Orleans jazz musicians had blown themselves out and eventually expired, there was nothing else to be done except produce faithful imitations. This was rarely attempted by young black musicians, who had turned to much more cerebral things, but instead by a breed of bibulous white musicians whose main affinity with the originals was that they could sink a fair quantity of liquor.

US revival bands rejoiced in colourful names like the Yerba Buena Jazz Band and the State Street Stompers. However, British revivalists, lacking these affiliations but sensing that a river connection lent a certain something, concocted names like the Crane River Jazz Band and the Kennet and Avon Canal Footwarmers.

CHICAGO JAZZ

Once Fate Marable had fleeced them of their fares upriver, most jazzmen got off the boat somewhere around St Louis, bought a hamburger with what they had left, then hitched a lift to Chicago. The place was so full of jazz musicians blowing themselves silly in the 1920s that its 'Windy City' moniker became even more appropriate.

The black musicians were mainly employed by one **Joe Oliver,** known as 'King' Oliver because he got there first. He was so paranoid that he played with a handkerchief over his hand to prevent people from copying his fingering. Oliver formed a group which he called his Creole Jazz Band (although it didn't seem to have any Creoles in it) and sent for an up-and-coming young cornetist called **Louis Armstrong** to join him (he wasn't a Creole either).

The first great Chicago jazz innovation was seen when the band, playing New Orleans sort of stuff, appeared with two cornets. Purists see this as the first step in the decline of jazz and towards the unfortunate excesses of the swing era. But the far-seeing bluffer should latch on to this and possibly start an argument about which bits Armstrong played and which bits Oliver took. The quality of the recordings makes it hard to tell, so it is a good area in which to turn hypothesis into bold assertion, in true bluffing tradition.

The other brand of Chicago jazz was that purveyed by white musicians. There were the professionals who modelled themselves on Oliver, calling their band the New Orleans Rhythm Kings; and there were the young lads, barely out of short trousers, who modelled their band on the New Orleans Rhythm Kings and called themselves the Chicagoans.

Not having the physical capacity of the regulars, they found the New Orleans style of playing, where everybody kept going all the time, a little taxing. So they invented a new Chicago style where they each took turns to play solos while the others had a drink or a drag, only combining briefly at the beginning and the end of a number. Some of them, like Pee Wee Russell, evolved very economical styles with a minimum of notes. As most jazz haunts in Chicago were boozing dives run by pushy businessmen such as Al Capone and his henchmen, the jazz musicians reckoned they were doing okay if they just kept playing and ignored the shooting. Bass players were particularly vulnerable, presenting as they did such large targets.

NEW YORK JAZZ

For various reasons, such as having a difference of opinion with Al Capone, jazz musicians gradually drifted towards New York, the city known as the Big Apple (because a lot of sinners wanted to take a bite out of it). So many black people moved into town that they took over most of the northern bit of Manhattan called Harlem, and that's where jazz really began (according to the stance that you choose to adopt). This is precarious ground for bluffers but you should be reasonably safe if you contend that Harlem is where jazz largely 'developed' – for a period, anyway, and much the same could be said of anywhere (even London).

Not only did bands have two cornets but they now played trumpets, sometimes three or four of them; and (whisper it not on Purity Street) saxophones – hundreds of them. The saxophone gradually came to epitomise jazz and gave it a bad name in conservative circles. Saxophones did not just blow or get blown – they honked and wailed and slapped and upset all right-thinking folk. The dustcart ensembles of New Orleans and the neurotic amateurism of the Chicagoans were ironed out in New York. The black musicians played a sort of 'mainstream' jazz long before the word was invented. It was a more professional kind of music in which all the musicians played cleverly (i.e., wandered beyond the three basic chords) and quite fast. Someone from Kansas City dropped in and showed them what a riff was, so they were all very happy.

Coleman 'The Hawk' Hawkins, the famous tenor saxophonist, later said that he didn't think there was any distinctive New York style and, so far as what was played in Harlem was concerned, he was right. But there was another sort of New York jazz that was played by the young white musicians who had come up in sax player Frankie 'Tram'

Trumbauer's car from Chicago. This was a stultified form of Chicago jazz played in a jerky sort of way that was much copied by British dance bands. The New York bands had names like Miff Mole and his Little Molers, Red Nichols and his Five Pennies and, just to confuse jazz chroniclers even more, the Original Memphis Five, The Charleston Chasers, the Louisiana Rhythm Kings, The Tennessee Tooters, the Savannah Six and the Cotton Pickers. Not to mention Gene Fosdick's Hoosiers or Fred 'Sugar' Hall and his Sugar Babies – in fact, thinking about it, they are very rarely mentioned.

Minton's Playhouse – which you will always succinctly refer to as Minton's – was in a disused china warehouse on West 118th Street in Harlem. A Christian sect (believers in guitarist **Charlie Christian,** a name that all bluffers should commit to memory) began holding meetings there around 1940, after they had reached the conviction that the sort of jazz that people could understand easily, could dance to and could simply enjoy had been going on quite long enough. It was time, they averred, that something was done about it!

To be fair, that wasn't actually Charlie Christian's own philosophy; he was quite content simply to be the best jazz guitarist ever and to play for his own pleasure at every opportunity, even if it was with a big commercial band. To that end he dispensed with all non-essentials, like food and sleep, dying in 1942 at the age of 25, thus providing another of the great dividing lines in jazz history: BC, or Before Christian.

Everything later than that is defined as AD, which stands for After Dizzy. **Dizzy Gillespie** was a jazz trumpet player (as if you didn't know) and among the most significant of all the Minton's habitués. Another was **Kenny 'Klook' Clarke** who had a way of whacking the bass drum at moments in the music when people were least expecting it. This made him very famous and, since war was just becoming fashionable again, the practice was known as dropping bombs. Just how many musicians were lost to us after suffering ruptured tympanic membranes (followed by cardiac arrest) is not recorded.

Besides creating a boom (in the other sense) in the sale and repair of bass-drum pedals, it put older musicians off their stroke (or beat), which was what some historians claim was the whole object of those sessions at Minton's. Kenny Clarke's bomb-dropping and the very complex harmonics and chords that Dizzy Gillespie and the jazz pianist **Thelonious Monk** worked out, together with the frantic tempos all the young musicians would indulge in, were believed to be part of a deliberate plan to drive non-progressive musicians (such as Louis Armstrong and all those white players like Benny Goodman who were making a lot of money out of jazz) off the stand. The fact that this has often been denied by those involved lends great weight and authority to the theory.

Thelonious Monk was such a weird cat that even other weird cats noticed it. His name, to start with, seems to have been partially created by himself, for there is evidence to suggest that his given first name was Thelius (which would have been quite odd enough for some people) and that his middle name, Sphere, was entirely of his own invention. He had a very accessible, completely beguiling and rather humorous style of playing which would occasionally take on the characteristics of ye olde stride piano with a sort of limp.

Many of the more academically correct pianists in jazz used to say that Monk couldn't play – so you can tell from that how extremely good and important he really was. He wore strange hats, had a wife named Nellie who cut his fingernails, and used words like 'crepuscule'.

Legendary sax-man **Charlie Parker** was a frequent sitter-in at Minton's but he wasn't strictly a Mintonian since his style had developed quite independently, largely in people's woodsheds and from listening to slowed-down Lester Young records. Nevertheless, Parker's presence on the scene was a great advantage because it has since given every musician who was around at that time the chance to claim that Charlie Parker once shared a room with him.

In fact, it's a pretty safe bet, if an unfamiliar 1940s/1950s name crops up in conversation, that you can easily get away with saying: 'Oh, yes. Parker roomed with him for a time.' Even if he didn't, nobody is going to be sure enough to say so. And it somehow makes the unknown musician seem a better player.

To sum up: Minton's was the place where modern jazz was invented. The fact that nearly 50 years have gone by since it happened means that it isn't strictly modern at all. But, just as in history the Middle Ages aren't anywhere near the middle, so in jazz the nomenclatures tend to slip a bit. This is to everyone's advantage, since it offers limitless opportunities to argue over what to call everything that has happened ever since, so feel free to go ahead and do just that.

KANSAS CITY JAZZ

This was rather like black New York jazz except that the Kansas jazzmen were hooked on riffs. A riff occurs when a musician finds a phrase that he likes, plays it until the others in the band pick it up, and then they keep on playing it in a compulsively propulsive (some might say 'mind-numbing') sort of way throughout the piece. The theory is that it came about one day when the needle got stuck in a groove, and those gathered about the phonograph were gripped by the novel effect. This is good bluffing material, insofar as it is impossible to prove wrong.

Kansas City jazz was mainly run by a man named Bennie Moten, later succeeded by Count Basie, who kept the riff tradition going strong for many lucrative years. Another KC bandleader was Jay McShann, who became a significant figure in jazz history because it was within the ranks of his outfit that Charlie Parker first had trouble with his reeds.

THE MODERN ERA

INTO THE COOL

What Cole Porter said about a 'crazy fling' of a love affair holds good for jazz as well: it was too hot not to cool down. The wonder is, in fact, that jazz managed to stay hot for as long as it did. In New Orleans it was kept at a steady 86°F, not difficult way down there since the state of Louisiana was part of Dixieland where, if it's true what they say, the sun really does shine all the time. Nor was it any problem making sure it stayed piping hot on the long trip 'up the river' (ensure that you have committed that phrase to memory). Jazz, along with its musicians, was stowed in the riverboat below the bilge next to the boiler room. And, in any case, Fate Marable crammed so many passengers, dancers, gamblers and other revellers aboard the riverboats that these iconic vessels, to quote a contemporary account, 'were not so much pleasure steamers as floating armpits'. Even when it got to the Windy City of Chicago, jazz remained a hot property in every sense. Most of the inhabitants were terrified of the gangsters, particularly Al Capone. The rival gangs would make gin in their bathtubs, beer in the garage and wine in army surplus wellingtons – hence the name 'bootleg'. This is only partly true, the name originally thought to have come about from hiding contraband in the legs of long boots in eighteenth-century Britain. But it's worth a good bluff nonetheless. It was the aim of each gang to hold a monopoly on the supply of their illegal but nutritious beverages. To that end they shot each other – and anybody else who looked as if they might know the secret of fermentation – on sight. Jazz musicians are born knowing the secret of fermentation, so, in order to keep alive, they had to present a constantly moving target. Neither they nor the music, therefore, had a chance to settle for a minute. This kept Chicago jazz, in particular, 'hot' and gave it its agitated character. Its temperature couldn't be brought down straight away, even when it arrived in north-easterly New York. Anyone who has ever been to the Big Apple knows that even the tiniest crack in the sidewalk has steam coming out of it.

The New York basements in which jazz flourished in the 1930s and 1940s were infamously stifling, but at least they were relatively safe from Capone and his henchmen. Jazz, once again, had little chance to get cooled to the point where it was fit for the table.

In 1949 it was decided that if jazz (which had been called 'hot' music since even before Jelly Roll Morton dreamed that he had invented it in 1902) was not disposed to obey the law of thermodynamics of its own accord, then it must be made to do so. The result was one of the two things in the history of the world ever to be successfully brought about by a committee. The first was the King James Bible; the second was the convincing of the general public that jazz, like dry sherry, ought to be served chilled.

The following are names that you must toss into any discussion of this aspect of jazz: **Gil Evans** (born in Canada – another useful card to have up your sleeve); **John Lewis** (who would later invent the Modern Jazz Quartet and who dressed in a manner that would have been approved of by Lord Reith); **Gerry Mulligan** (who invented the Gerry Mulligan Quartet and had a tendency to dress like Hamlet) and **Johnny Carisi** (a trumpet player who had never been heard of before and has never been seen since). They were the Cooling Committee. The committee passed a resolution and co-opted **Miles Davis,** who immediately took over and became the dominant element in the nine-piece band specially assembled for Operation Frigidaire.

In 1949 the band was booked for two weeks at a venue called the Royal Roast in Harlem. In view of its declared aims, this name was felt to be something of an ill omen, and the management was persuaded to change it to the Royal Roost, which explains how this otherwise inexplicable name came into the history books. (State with confidence that it might have been a chicken restaurant.) Casually referred to as the Royal Roost band (use the name at every opportunity), it did a couple of recording sessions and, when the results were put together, the album was called *Birth of the Cool* so that there should be absolutely no mistake about what they were trying to do.

Thus the cool school was founded, and eager pupils

hurried to enrol. One of its housemasters was blind pianist Lennie Tristano, who taught the joint head prefects of the school, the alto saxophonist Lee Konitz and the tenor-saxophonist Warne Marsh, whose first name was a clever amalgamation of 'wan' and 'worn', a reflection of the

---

♔

A much hotter form of cool jazz was started up called 'hard bop' – because it was hard to play and, for some people, even harder to listen to.

---

way some say he sounded. Soon after, this cool school opened up a branch in California, paradoxically because the weather was warmer there. It was called West Coast jazz and gave jazz people an interesting topic: discussing whether West Coast jazz was cooler and more intellectual than the East Coast variety. Meanwhile, inevitably, a reaction had set in, and a much hotter form of cool jazz was started up called 'hard bop' – because it was hard to play and, for some people, even harder to listen to.

Hard bop musicians included the drummer Art Blakey, who had metal studs which were named after him nailed to the bottom of his boots. State with a straight face that this was the beginning of 'sole' music. As time has gone by, so it has become more apparent that many of the cool players were in reality pretty hot, while several of the hard boppers were really cool and cognisant – a pretty cerebral lot. In fact, the further you get away from the 1950s and 1960s, the harder it becomes to see what all the fuss was about, leaving you to wonder, once again, if it was the writers who cranked up a lot of jazz history as a precaution against redundancy. Furthermore, if there is ever a lull in the conversation, you can always get it going again by pointing out that the first cool jazz musician was actually Bix Beiderbecke, in the late 1920s, but everybody was too busy enjoying the music and dodging Al Capone to notice it at the time.

BEBOP, OR BOP, AND HARD BOP

Bebop is the frighteningly athletic modern jazz movement that began when musicians started ignoring the melody (when there was one) and used the chords as a very rough guide to what they were doing, usually trying to show how fast they could play. They have been doing the same ever since. Musical conservatives described bebop as 'musical communism', which makes Charlie Parker bebop's Marx, Lenin and Trotsky all rolled into one. You will get extra bluffing points if you insist that the Coleman Hawkins solo on *Body And Soul* was the prototype for bebop improvisation.

Confusingly, hard bop isn't actually that hard to bop to. It is usually quite a bit easier than straight bop (or bebop), both to play and to listen to. Initially a reaction to bebop's airy intellectualism, hard bop is the funky, bluesy, gospel-influenced jazz that you hear being used on dozens of TV theme tunes and ads – something that has kept a host of grizzled old jazz musicians in modest luxury for many years. (The bop-phobic critic Stanley Dance once wrote that he was relatively unworried by hard bop because if it fell to the floor it would very likely be smashed to smithereens; a phenomenon described as soft bop was more of a worry, though, because of the mess it could make.)

FREEFORM

This is the crazy, anything-goes world of totally free improvisation, cranking the harmonic freedom of bebop up a few notches. Initially it comprised a few African-American musicians solemnly claiming it as a break from 'European' notions of melody and harmony, using instruments as a source of unusual sounds as much as a melodic device. Before long it became a way of hiding the fact that you couldn't play your instrument properly. Musicians who took the time and trouble to play their instruments properly dismissed this sort of stuff as 'fire in a pet shop' or 'chicken-choking'. Note that chicken metaphors are very prevalent in jazz circles. Feel free to resort to them at any time.

It's important to observe the correct code of behaviour at a freeform concert, if you can ever be persuaded to go. Nod politely with your eyes shut. Smile or laugh at inappropriate intervals: this will suggest that you've tapped into some complex avant-garde joke that no one else comprehends. Don't, whatever you do, applaud when the saxophonist drops his instrument on his foot, although it's often easy to confuse these sounds with the rattling, squawking and banging that constitute the performance.

FUSION

Originally an abbreviation of 'jazz-rock fusion', this is now a rather lazy catch-all term for the kind of hyphenated jazz which sees musicians trying to fuse jazz improvisation with Indian classical music, Afro-Cuban salsa, Brazilian bossa nova, West African juju, Argentine tango, Indonesian gamelan, Welsh male voice choirs and so on. Some people have become so bewildered that they think that jazz is a form of salsa invented in Wales by Nigerian gamelan performers. Cynics refer to the resulting sound as confusion, with the emphasis on the con.

ECM

You could describe ECM as a label for people who don't like music but this might be a little unfair. ECM – Edition of Contemporary Music – was founded in 1969 by a German hippy called Manfred Eicher. Initially a classical record producer, Eicher wanted to recreate the ambience of a classical session for jazz improvisers. Before long he had found a home for the likes of Keith Jarrett, Chick Corea, Pat Metheny, John Abercrombie, Jan Garbarek, Kenny Wheeler and many more besides. The jazz bluffer should display strong opinions about ECM's output. You must either praise it to the skies as a really significant jazz development or decry it as soulless, ambient mush for the hippy-dippy New Age movement. There's no room here for equivocation.

LE JAZZ HOT

Was this a jazz movement or not? Was it a seminal development in the history of jazz? Did it exist? Does anyone know? No one knows anything about Le Jazz Hot, apart from possibly a few French jazz enthusiasts who almost certainly know nothing about it either, so make up as much as you want about it with impunity. But stick to the few facts that are known. It is thought to be linked to the city of Paris, specifically to a jazz group known as Le Quintette du Hot Club de France. This was founded by Belgian jazz guitarist Django Reinhardt (1910-1953) and violinist Stéphane Grapelli (1908-1997) in the 1930s and was disbanded in the late 1940s. Some say that it was one of the most significant and innovative jazz bands in the history of recorded jazz, but they were probably French or Belgian. If the subject comes up, nod sagely and say: 'Astonishing thing about Django. He had only two working fingers on his left hand as a result of being caught in a caravan fire in his teens. Did you know he was a Romany?'

Then you can go on to talk with authority about how Django invented a whole new musical sub-genre known as Le Gypsy Jazz. If pressed, say confidently: 'And that is how Le Jazz Hot came into being.' No one could possibly disagree with you.

HORN BLOWERS

I f you've managed to stay with us up to this point, you will be aware that jazz, its evolution and essence (a phrase borrowed from a book of the same name by André Hodeir), are dependent mainly on the people who actually make the music. The preceding paragraphs are dotted with a modest litany of such artists, but this is where that list needs to be expanded a little. The earnest jazz fan throws names about like confetti, and the bluffer is advised to do likewise.

Most of the well-known names are now dead, which could be just as well because they are no longer around to answer back or threaten legal action. It might be logical to start with cornet and trumpet players because, traditionally, they tended to be at the front and in the middle.

CORNET AND TRUMPET PLAYERS

LOUIS 'SATCHMO' ARMSTRONG (1901–1971)

Undeniably a genius and universally recognised as one of the greatest of all jazz musicians, Louis Armstrong also had one of the most gravelly voices. Attempts were made to consolidate his greatness by altering the record of his birth to make it appear that he was born on Independence Day in 1900; his actual birthdate was the more mundane 4 August 1901.

Two things the bluffer must do are, first, to state unequivocally that his finest work came in the 1920s, citing his cornet playing on 'West End Blues' and 'Potato Head Blues'; second, that his tragedy was that he got rich by singing songs like 'Hello, Dolly!' and the undiluted saccharin of 'What a Wonderful World'. Genuine jazz lovers will see you straight away as a kindred spirit. They might even begin to think you're more than that if you commit two riveting pieces of trivia to memory: first, ol' Satchmo's nickname was a truncated version of the less than flattering soubriquet 'Satchelmouth' and, second, he consumed a daily dose of a ferocious herbal laxative called Swiss Kriss.

BIX BEIDERBECKE (1903–1931)

Another cornet player who became a jazz legend in the 1920s, Bix was a dedicated alcoholic who died young after a brief career playing in large bands led by Jean Goldkette, Frankie Trumbauer and Paul Whiteman. He had a bell-like singing tone, as smooth as a Speyside single malt that shone through some turgid musical mud like a good deed in a naughty world. At the mention of his name you should nod sagely and murmur 'Singin' the Blues' and 'I'm comin', Virginia' in tones of reverence. As a conversational bonus you could mention 'In a Mist', Bix's mystical piano solo which owed quite a lot to Debussy. Sadly, Debussy died in 1918, too soon to collect his dues.

CHARLES 'BUDDY' BOLDEN (1877–1931)

Lurking in the shadows of early jazz history was this character, known as the Demon Barber of Bourbon Street. Many myths surrounded his existence, most of them emanating from the shaky memory and dubious imagination of those such as Bunk Johnson (*see* below). Scholarly research has dispelled such fictions, though what is left is the vague possibility that he played the cornet the wrong way round (there is photographic evidence of this), and you'll recall that when he blew it the right way round it could be heard up to 14 miles away. This depended on what he'd been drinking before he blew, and on what the listener had been drinking before he thought he heard it.

WILLIAM GEARY 'BUNK' JOHNSON (1889–1949)

Various people have attempted to muddy the waters of jazz history, notoriously this veteran New Orleans trumpet player. Bunk confused early historians by making various adjustments to the truth, including the date of his own birth, and ever since then, much energy and time has been expended in trying set the record straight.

In 1933 dental problems caused Bunk to stop playing and he vanished from the jazz scene to become, it is said, a fairground whistler – quite a challenge for a man minus teeth. He was rediscovered in 1939 by a group of enthusiasts for early jazz, probably dedicated enough to chip in for some dentistry and a trumpet. Together with some other veterans he made a few records which went a long way to confirming what the cynics believed: that genuine New Orleans jazz was rough stuff and hardly ever in tune, but even they had to admit it possessed integrity.

ORIGINAL DIXIELAND JAZZ BAND

The first jazz records ever made, in 1917, were the work of the all-white Original Dixieland Jazz Band, whose 'Livery Stable Blues' was reckoned to have launched the Jazz Age. In 1919 the band came to London, making yet more records, and playing at Buckingham Palace at the invitation of King George V, who was reported to be favourably impressed. Leading this pioneering assembly was Nick LaRocca (1889-1961), a brash cornet player who not only played in the band but also wrote tunes for it that frequently turned out to have been written by someone else – 'Tiger Rag', for example. When the ODJB was revived in 1936 and made some records, it came as a great relief to many, proving as it did that the band sounded so odd in its early manifestation only because of the primitive equipment of the time. In any reference to its first recording, you should state with some authority that the band's cornetist Freddie Keppard initially refused to be recorded on the perfectly understandable grounds that other musicians might steal his ideas.

ERNEST LORING NICHOLS (1905–1965)

Fortunately for Nichols, he had red hair and so did not have to suffer being called either Ernest or Loring, both being such unjazzy names, and was instead able to answer to 'Red'. He led a New York dixie-style band called the Five Pennies (five pennies equalling a nickel, an amusing play on his surname which you doubtless spotted). He took liberties with the maths because the band could consist of between six and 10 players, with himself leading on cornet. He is often unjustly dismissed as a pale imitator of Bix. Hollywood immortalised him with a film based on his life, starring another redhead: Danny Kaye, no less.

FRANCIS 'MUGGSY' SPANIER (1906–1967)

Many people thought Spanier was called Muggsy because he had what could be described as a homely face – slightly squashed, slightly sad-looking – but he insisted that such was not the case. Nevertheless, the name suits him to a T. His cornet style was warm, almost conversational, often with a plunger mute. His greatest claim to fame was to lead a Dixieland group called the Ragtime Band, conveniently overlooking the fact that it wasn't a ragtime band at all. In 1939 this band made a set of recordings, each of such joyous excellence that they became known as 'The Great 16'. One of the greatest of the great was 'Relaxin' at the Touro', a tribute to the New Orleans infirmary where Spanier received treatment for the scourge of many a jazzman, a fondness for the bottle.

JOHN BIRKS 'DIZZY' GILLESPIE (1917–1993)

There's no proof that NASA designed a trumpet for John Gillespie, but there's no proof to the contrary either, so give it a whirl. Diz wanted the horn to point upwards to disseminate the sound more effectively in low-ceilinged venues.

He was a founding father of the goatee-beard school of jazz, which convened at Minton's, and he is hailed along with Charlie Parker and others as a high priest of beboppery. Having long overstrained his cheek muscles, he always looked to be on the point of bursting, but was thus able to blow as many as 36 fairly high and rapid notes with one puff. But who's counting?

MILES DAVIS (1926–1991)

During his lifetime, Miles Davis put up with racial prejudice, insults, misunderstandings, a heroin habit and withdrawal from it, prolonged illness, a lot of pain, immoderate adulation and barrow loads of money. Otherwise he led a fairly uneventful life. He wasn't a particularly popular figure with audiences, promoters, some personal acquaintances and a handful of fellow musicians. Like many a genius, Miles (always called Miles) was as cuddly as a cactus. Any conversation about him starts from the assumption that, no matter what his musical circumstances, the actual trumpet playing always remained the same. Question this and you could be asking for trouble. You could actually do yourself a bit of good by casually pointing out that Miles was about the only jazz musician whose audiences got younger as he got older, thanks to his cunning scheme of playing grown-up jazz at 19, jazz-rock at 39 and straight rock at 59. Early on he became notorious for turning his back on the audience, and by the mid-1980s he had adopted the ploy of walking slowly backwards on-stage, bent nearly double, scattering little slivers of melody as he did so. This curious conduct may be completely without significance, but don't be deterred from indulging in a spot of psychological speculation.

TROMBONISTS

Now it's time for a modest inventory of trombonists. The word 'trombone' is derived from the Italian, meaning 'large trumpet', though this etymological nicety is unlikely to have figured too prominently in the minds of early jazzmen. Their principal concern would be the need for plenty of room in which to play it, especially when the slide was extended to arm's length. Bands would often travel around town on the back of a truck to advertise a forthcoming engagement. The trombonist would be banished to the back of the vehicle, blowing out over the tailgate. Hence the term 'tailgate' for this vigorous style of playing with its rhythmic emphasis, exemplified in a piece like 'Ory's Creole Trombone', named after its composer and most famous performer, Edward 'Kid' Ory (1886-1973). He featured on many classic recordings with both Louis Armstrong and Jelly Roll Morton.

JACK TEAGARDEN (1905-1964)

Another highly rated and influential trombonist who worked with Armstrong was Jack Teagarden, whose playing and singing were both strongly tinged with a Texan drawl, and who sounded as though he enjoyed a perpetual hangover. Point out that he was regarded by some as a white man's answer to Louis Armstrong, and frequently duetted with the maestro, notably in Hoagy Carmichael's classic 'Rockin' Chair'. Such was his modesty that when he appeared as the guest on Desert Island Discs, all eight of his record choices featured him.

Some trombonists were inclined to defy the limitations of the instrument, playing so that notes poured forth in such profusion that it might as well be a trumpet. Examples include Jimmy Cleveland (1926-2008) and Dane Kai Winding (1922-1983), who recorded some duets with JJ Johnson (1924-2001). Billed as 'Jay & Kai' they sounded at times like musical machine-guns.

MIKE ZWERIN (1930-2010)

One trombonist was famous for his desire to rattle out notes at high speed, so much so that he set aside the instrument and settled for a curiosity called a bass trumpet. He was Mike Zwerin, who became even more famous for always being the last entry in alphabetical listings in jazz reference books.

CLARINETTISTS

BENNY GOODMAN (1909-1986)

Among jazz clarinettists, perhaps the most famous and prolific was Benny Goodman, who was crowned King of Swing in 1935 at a dignified ceremony attended only by his manager, his agent, his bank manager and Pee Wee Russell, who hadn't the faintest idea as to why he was there. News of the coronation drew immense crowds of besotted subjects to all future Goodman concerts. There were some individuals who grumbled behind Goodman's throne, especially Paul Whiteman, who had only recently been crowned King of Jazz and thought that as a fellow monarch he might at least have been consulted. Other dissenters were a handful of other bandleaders who wished they'd had the idea first.

WOODROW CHARLES HERMAN (1913–1987)

Another clarinet-playing bandleader was Woodrow Charles Herman, better known, inevitably, as 'Woody'. He rather cheekily referred to his musicians as being members of a herd, but they never appeared to mind. The First Herd was succeeded by the Second, and the Second by the Third, and so on up to about Sixteen, at which point he didn't seem to bother any more. In 1939 he had tremendous success with a simple number called 'Woodchopper's Ball'. This helped raise woodchoppers in the esteem of the US public. 'Woodchopper's' was a great number,' Woody was reported as saying resignedly, 'the first thousand times we played it.'

MILTON 'MEZZ' MEZZROW (1899–1972)

One of the oddest characters among the cast of clarinet players, Mezz was probably better known as co-author of a memoir of remarkable frankness called *Really the Blues,* in which he made it plain that though he was white he would prefer to be black. As a player he was more enthusiastic than actually musical, but delivered the goods adequately on some historic recordings with trumpet player Tommy Ladnier. However, he was more than adequate when it came to the delivery of other goods, namely narcotics, which made him rather popular in some circles.

CHARLES ELLSWORTH 'PEE WEE' RUSSELL (1906–1969)

The word 'unique' is hard to avoid when it comes to the consideration of Pee Wee Russell, and that could be applied to his looks every bit as much as to his clarinet playing. His face was long and not unlike a rueful bloodhound, and his tone was broken every so often by a croak, as if the instrument was a martyr to bronchitis. But he made the most miraculous music, highly individual and inventive, surprising and spontaneous, as though Thelonious Monk had taken up the clarinet. He was a true jazz eccentric – rather wonderful, and burdened with a name like Ellsworth, who could blame him for answering to Pee Wee?

SAX APPEAL

Shunned as an outcast in the early days, the saxophone has become probably the most widely acknowledged instrument in the jazz locker. Conjecture that this is perhaps because of its range and variety, from rumbling bass to silvery sopranino – though you'd be hard-pressed to find either of these two in a band these days. Another reason for the ubiquity of the saxophone, usually the tenor, could be that most women are beguiled by its qualities, thus making it the musical equivalent of the E-Type Jaguar.

♔

One of the reasons for the ubiquity of the saxophone, usually the tenor, could be that most women are beguiled by its qualities, thus making it the musical equivalent of the E-Type Jaguar.

COLEMAN HAWKINS (1901–1969)

While Louis Armstrong was the cream of the jazz crop, everybody was trying to copy him, and then along came Coleman Hawkins wielding the newfangled saxophone, recently invented (in 1846). He set out to show the jazz world a new way of doing things altogether, consolidating his supremacy with a stunning version of 'Body and Soul'. Often referred to as 'Bean', an allusion to his broad tone, or as 'Hawk' or 'The Hawk', which is obvious.

WILLIAM 'RED' MCKENZIE (1899–1948)

In 1929 Hawk played on one of the happiest recordings ever: 'Hello Lola' by the Mound City Blue Blowers. The leader was Red McKenzie, the only virtuoso performer on comb-and-paper, a sort of cousin to the saxophone as the paper could be loosely defined as a reed. McKenzie became a household name for a while, but is mainly remembered fondly by musicians as one who found jobs for the boys during the Depression years.

SIDNEY BECHET (1897–1969)

Nobody ever had a problem with identifying the sound of Sidney Bechet on the soprano saxophone, with its forceful projection and vigorous vibrato. To see why, just listen to 'Nobody Knows the Way I Feel this Morning' (1940).

BENNY CARTER (1907–2003)

One of the most versatile of musicians, Benny Carter played not only tenor and alto saxophones, but also clarinet, trumpet and trombone, resisting any temptation to play them all at the same time. Carter was a fine arranger too – almost in the same league as Duke Ellington – though you might observe sadly that his arrangement of 'The Teddy Bears' Picnic' for Henry Hall and the BBC Dance Orchestra (1932) should not be considered as one of his more distinguished works.

LAWRENCE 'BUD' FREEMAN (1906–1991)

It is said that someone once commented to Bud Freeman, 'You look like a doctor but you play like a murderer.' It is certainly true that he dressed in a dapper fashion (he once did a one-off modelling job on the strength of it) and played in a huffing and puffing manner like a big bad wolf. His style on tenor saxophone was entirely his own creation, with a vibrato-like washing flapping in the breeze. He was that rarity, a Chicago jazzman actually born in Chicago. The most important thing to seize on is whether or not he was an influence on Lester Young. You can take either view, for it is difficult to tell.

LESTER YOUNG (1909–1959)

Justly celebrated for being the coolest of the hot tenors, Lester Young took up the saxophone only because he saw his brother Lee miss the pick of the girls at a gig owing to the time it took to pack up his drum kit. Lester was almost as famous for his pork-pie hats, which he even wore in bed. He was the last of the saxophonists to please Hugues Panassié (an influential French jazz critic of the time) because he swung and played in a melodic manner, and the first to please the modernists because he paved the way to Parkerism. He did much of his best work in the Basie band, filling in the wide-open spaces between the notes the Count occasionally played. He was dubbed 'Pres' (short for President) by Billie Holiday, and you should always do the same.

ORNETTE COLEMAN (1930–)

Just as the cinema organ world seemed full of Reginalds, so is jazz heavily populated by Colemans: Coleman Hawkins, Bill Coleman, George Coleman, Earl Coleman, Leslie Coleman McCann (who pretends he isn't one by calling himself Les McCann), Oliver Coleman, Davie Coleman, Cy Coleman – not forgetting Cozy and Nat 'King' Cole, man. But the most controversial of them is

Ornette Coleman, so-called because the critics realised as soon as they heard him that they would be poking their typewriters into an ornette's nest of artistic discomfiture. Having been once bitten by Charlie Parker 16 years earlier, they were now twice as shy. Ornette played a plastic alto; he blew little bursts of often quite catchy melody; you couldn't count the bars but his drummers usually went tish-ti-tish as in the old days. Traditionalist listeners, recognising a fellow primitive, frequently took to him right away. Now that the term avant-garde has fallen out of favour, Ornette (which is the bit of the name you use, even if it sounds a bit effeminate) has become almost an establishment figure, currently using an orthodox metal saxophone – though he calls what he plays on it 'harmolodic' music, and nobody knows what that means. He still plays violin occasionally, although he might be better advised not to.

JOHN COLTRANE (1926–1967)

The fact that most jazz saxophone playing since the 1960s has had a granite-like hardness can be blamed on John Coltrane. A 1950s junkie (it is safe to assume that everybody was supported by something at that time, even if it was only by Dr J Collis Browne's chlorodyne mixture for gippy stomachs), musical dedication and iron discipline enabled him to kick the habit in 1957. Then he discovered God and the harp. At the same time he created a style of playing called Sheets of Sound. It was coined to describe Coltrane's wish to exhaust the possibilities of every tune he tackled by not only playing the relevant notes but every note of every related scale, more or less all at once. It needed a clever person to do it, and another to invent such a nicely ambiguous name. Use it whenever you can and never forget to refer to Coltrane as 'Trane'.

GERRY MULLIGAN (1927–1996)

Until the late 1940s some jazz popularity polls tended to designate the baritone saxophone as 'miscellaneous instrument'. Then Gerry Mulligan turned up, and with a combination of delicate puffing and nimble fingering he gained recognition for the instrument in its own right. With equally nimble footwork he kicked the piano to one side, forming a historic and popular quartet consisting only of baritone, trumpet, bass and drums that made a wonderful sound – cool but not cold. Pianists sulked as he gained fame and a measure of prosperity, though he did appease them to some extent by occasionally playing the piano himself. His nickname was 'Jeru', which nobody ever used except him, when he wrote a piece of music with that title. You should never use it either, but be on the lookout for its careless use by others and chalk it up against them.

CHARLIE 'YARDBIRD' PARKER (1920–1956)

Alto player Charlie Parker was the first jazz musician to be elected to the Wall of Fame. Within hours of his last breath, the legend 'BIRD LIVES!' had been daubed on the walls of the New York subway. Although he died, as one commentator said, 'of everything', he was now officially immortal. In fact, after Louis Armstrong, he is the most immortal jazz person you will have to bluff about. He didn't quite start modern jazz single-handedly because there were others around at the time, like Dizzy Gillespie and Thelonious Monk, who were involved as well. Parker's contribution was to play well-known pop tunes so fast and so brilliantly that no one could recognise them. He also gave them new titles, which confused everyone still further. It's worth noting that 'Cherokee' by Ray Noble (who was born in Brighton) became 'Koko' by Charlie Parker (who wasn't); Duke Ellington wrote an entirely different 'Koko', which begins to look like a conspiracy, causing Ray Noble to fret until the end of his days. Charlie Parker had a New York club named after him, Birdland, which became so full even he couldn't get in.

WALTER 'SONNY' ROLLINS (1930–)

You can stall for time when bluffing about Sonny Rollins by pondering his best haircut. Was it his early-'60s mohawk, his terrifying mid-'60s skinhead, his Afro in the 1970s? You should also insist that he was the model for Bleeding Gums Murphy, the grizzled old saxophonist in *The Simpsons*. You can rhapsodise about how Rollins is the only saxophonist who doesn't necessarily need a backing band.

THEY GOT RHYTHM

Bluffers will know that the rhythm section of a jazz band comprises bass, drums, guitar and, not always but generally, the piano.

WILLIAM 'COUNT' BASIE (1904–1984)

In spite of Al Capone and Gerry Mulligan's best efforts to dispense with it, the old joanna remains a significant instrument in jazz, played in a bewildering variety of styles. The leading exponent of the less-is-more school was Count Basie. His piano playing became more sparse as he grew older, so that during the last years of his life he played fewer notes but more music, giving rise to the slogan: 'The less he played, the more he conveyed.' He also led one of the most infectiously swinging bands of all time, unleashing the full power of combined brass and reeds by raising a single finger.

EDWARD KENNEDY 'DUKE' ELLINGTON (1899–1974)

Another piano-playing nobleman at the court of jazz was Duke Ellington, who actually managed to keep a big band going from the early 1920s to the time of his death. He was a fine and flamboyant pianist, but say that his true instrument was his orchestra. This will make them sit up and take notice. Continue by pointing out that his reputation was established by supplying so-called 'jungle' music for the well-heeled (white) clientele of the Cotton Club in Harlem. One school of thought asserts that the Duke's creative peak was reached in the 1940s, but his achievements before and since were hardly less elevated, though he did suffer from the occasional lapse in musical judgment.

EARL HINES (1903–1983)

Bearing another noble name (but from birth), Earl Hines had no need of a purloined title to underpin his grand status. Indeed, he preferred a measure of humility and became popularly known as 'Fatha'. He invented the 'trumpet' style of piano, playing notes simultaneously an octave apart to help them penetrate the primitive recording equipment of the 1920s. He contrived to keep his playing fresh and original, using up to 57 different varieties of approach.

THOMAS 'FATS' WALLER (1904–1943)

Larger than life is a rather understated description of Fats Waller, who weighed in at about 24 stone and strove valiantly to keep it that way with a truly astonishing intake of food and alcohol. He was a merry musical alchemist, turning some of Tin Pan Alley's basest metals into gold with his piano playing, which was brilliant, and his warm-hearted and sometimes tender singing. Sadly, his gargantuan appetite was the death of him and he died aboard a train approaching Kansas.

LIONEL HAMPTON (1909–2002)

One of the lesser-known ivory ticklers. Lionel Hampton was a multi-instrumental genius who played the piano like a vibraphone, the vibraphone like a piano, the drums like mad and everything very loud and fast.

JAMES P JOHNSON (1894–1955)

In spite of looking like a boxing promoter, complete with cigar, James P Johnson was a brilliant pianist of the Harlem school who played with great delicacy and finesse.

ART TATUM (1909–1956)

If you depended on auditory evidence alone, you may be inclined to believe that Art Tatum possessed 12 fingers. Listen carefully to his records and you might hear faintly the piano begging for mercy, or at least a break. His mastery of the keyboard was all the more remarkable considering that he had been virtually blind since birth, and more remarkable still when you learn that he rarely played without the help of prodigious amounts of alcohol – which seemed to have absolutely no effect on his flawless execution of whatever he was playing. On the other hand, it was so fast that no one could tell if he was making mistakes or not (least of all himself).

HERBIE HANCOCK (1940–)

A pianist who always looks about 14 years old – and still tries to make music that appeals to 14-year-olds – is Herbie Hancock, the only leading jazz musician to have appeared on *Sesame Street* and composed the soundtrack for an animated TV children's show *(Fat Albert and the Cosby Kids).* You are allowed to dismiss most of his disco stuff of the 1970s and early 1980s, but be careful always to insist that his acoustic piano playing is 'pristine'.

That you find yourself bluffing about jazz at all could well be because of the existence of one or more of these four pianists: Oscar Peterson, John Lewis, Erroll Garner and Dave Brubeck. What each of them had in common was the ability, especially in the 1950s and 1960s, to persuade an immense audience that God would not smite them with a plague of boils if they went to a jazz concert. By becoming very popular and earning more than a bare living, these four offended many jazz purists who reached for their most potent and waspish insult: 'commercial'. It might be as well for you to gauge the attitude of your co-bluffers before you adopt a definite stance on these artists.

OSCAR PETERSON (1925–2007)

A useful point to remember about Oscar Peterson ('Oscar', or even plain 'Osc') is that he was born in Canada. He was physically very large, with hands in proportion, and only the huge Bösendorfer piano, with its extra notes at the bottom end, could accommodate his spread. He usually worked with a trio, which at one time included the bass player Niels-Henning Ørsted Pedersen (1946-2005), whose record for having the longest name in jazz still stands. Just for emergencies, keep handy the knowledge that Peterson's singing voice is uncannily like Nat 'King' Cole's – another 'commercial'.

JOHN LEWIS (1920-2001)

John Lewis is in an ambivalent position. In the early days, he played alongside Charlie Parker, which is as near as you can go in the jazz world to achieving sainthood. On the other hand, he helped dream up the idea of the Modern Jazz Quartet, soberly dressed as though for a funeral, playing elegantly swinging music which people could understand, and made a large amount of money as a result. You can tell what a questionable notion it was from the way it only managed to last from 1952 for something over 30 years – apart a brief hiatus in the 1970s.

ERROLL GARNER (1921-1977)

Most pianists grunt as they play, but Erroll Garner, known by some impertinent people as Ear'ole, played as he grunted – louder than just about anybody else. Nobody really minded because he swung like the proverbial old boots, in spite of a left hand that seemed to be loitering with intent. Audiences loved such a big personality in a man who was so small that he needed a Manhattan telephone directory to elevate him on the piano stool.

DAVE BRUBECK (1920–2012)

The leader of the eponymous quartet was another pianist who succeeded in attracting listeners to jazz in droves, though it is true to say that for every punter who came to tap a foot to Brubeck's keyboard work, a combination of the Gothic and the Baroque, there were two more who stayed to revel in the graceful, limpid alto saxophone playing of Paul Desmond (1924-1977). If you get the chance, make it plain that you know it was really Desmond who wrote 'Take Five', and not Brubeck as so widely believed.

While we're in the rhythm section, it would be wrong not to mention some of the great jazz drummers, even if most people with any sense of self-preservation live in mortal dread of being subjected to a jazz drum solo – or, to be fair, any drum solo in any musical genre. The ones you need to know about include:

ARTHUR 'ART' BLAKEY (1919–1990)

Also known as Abdullah Ibn Buhaina after converting to Islam, all you need to say about Art (or 'Bu' as he preferred to be known post-conversion) is that he was one of the pioneers of the newfangled bebop style of drumming. To the untrained ear it sounds exactly the same as any other style of drumming, but you must never admit to that.

BUDDY RICH (1917–1987)

And, of course, it would be impossible to have any sort of conversation about jazz drummers without mentioning

Buddy Rich. Given the birth name Bernard, and born into a Jewish vaudeville family in Brooklyn, Rich's talent was allegedly first spotted at the age of one by his father, who noticed that he was banging in perfect time with a couple of spoons. He made his first appearance on stage aged 18 months, and by 12 he was one of the highest-paid child performers in the world (an early recording of him drumming to 'Stars and Stripes Forever' can be heard on YouTube). Rich always claimed that he'd never received a drum lesson in his life. Some will say that it showed, but you will not be among them. In fact, you will say that he fully merited the description 'the world's greatest drummer', and venture that his proudest moment was in a 1981 episode of *The Muppet Show* where he took on the character Animal in a famous drum battle.

SONNY GREER (1895–1982)

You might also mention Sonny Greer, if only because he played with Duke Ellington in the Cotton Club and was a noted drum designer. In fact, he designed and used one of the biggest drum kits ever seen including chimes, gongs, timpani and vibes. Sadly, because of a drinking and gambling problem, his famous drum kits spent more time in the pawnshop than on stage.

And finally, we come to jazz guitar. Feel confident in stating that it starts with Django Reinhardt (1910-1953) and ends with Wes Montgomery (1923-1968) (*see* 'Need-to-know Albums'), with Charlie Christian (1916-1942) somewhere in between. That's really all you need to say.

This book makes no claims to be encyclopaedic or exhaustive. The intention is simply to supply a modest amount of ammunition and help bluffers baffle bluffers. However, there is one more name that merits inclusion before closing this section:

ALBERT EDWIN 'EDDIE' CONDON (1905–1973)

Known not so much for his musical contributions on guitar and banjo, but for his role as a facilitator, fixer and propagandist for unpretentious and wholesome jazz, often in public jam sessions, Eddie Condon had the knack of infusing participating musicians with tremendous energy and warmth, and there's a lot of evidence on record. He is also gratefully remembered for his hangover cure: 'Take the juice of two quarts of whiskey.'

OTHER JAZZ UTENSILS

Picture a smart luggage store in New York, some time in 1933 – a quiet place, the atmosphere heavy with the scent of new leather.

A serious-looking man enters the shop. His name is **Virgil Scoggins** (truly). A beaming salesman approaches, but before he can start his patter Virgil starts a patter of his own. Virgil is a suitcase virtuoso. He picks one up and slaps and taps it expertly, bending close in order to savour the tone, muttering and humming high and low. Customers and salesmen recognise the tune and la-la along. It's Gershwin's 'I Got Rhythm'. The performance is repeated until Virgil finds a case with all the desired musical qualities to blend with his band Spirits of Rhythm. Virgil and his case could be heard to excellent advantage on 'Brunswick 01715' (now sadly lost to posterity).

The percussion of the Spirits is not the only novel aspect of the group. The sound that identifies it is that of the 'tiple', an overfed ukelele from Hawaii with steel strings and a ringing tone, played without a plectrum. There were three of them in the Spirits line-up, plus the tasteful guitar of Teddy Bunn (1909-1978). The leader was Leo Watson (1898-1950), a prince among scat singers. Bonus bluffing points could be earned by letting slip that Leo was later recruited by Artie Shaw and sang thoughtful ballads like 'Shoot the Likker to Me John Boy'.

From the very earliest days, bands have plundered households to elevate mundane utensils to the status of musical instruments. This can be useful territory for the bluffer. Back in 1896, nearly 20 years before the word 'jazz' or 'jass' appeared, Albert 'Slew-Foot Pete' Montluzin, unable to afford the real thing, fashioned his guitar from a cigar box; Emile 'Whisky' Benrod cut a whiskey barrel in half to build a string bass; and Cleve 'Warm Gravy' Carven played a banjo, the body of which was once a cheese box. This sort of ingenuity was not unusual among the impoverished. Slew-Foot's uncle Esteban once reputedly made a cajón box drum out of a three-piece suite.

Red McKenzie's comb-and-paper has already been noted. The most diligent research has failed to reveal what sort of paper he preferred to generate that tuneful buzz. You might think about suggesting that the most likely stuff from that era would be that robust, old-fashioned toilet paper bearing the legend 'MEDICATED WITH IZAL GERMICIDE', printed in green.

Jugs and bottles were frequently diverted from their intended use to be blown across the top like an outsize pan pipe, serving as one-note tubas: thoom, thoom, thoom. Best known of the jug blowers was probably **Gus Cannon** (1883-1979), a man of the Mississippi who later moved to

Memphis and led a trio called Cannon's Jug Stompers. He was actually a banjo player who ingeniously mounted the jug on his left shoulder so that he could blow and pluck at the same time. Cannon's jug tone was deep and rich, the result of the vessel's previous contents. It was Napoleon brandy, which could explain why the band's records sold well in France, where Cannon was lionised as a 'Juggiste' par excellence.

It was the domestic laundry that furnished a couple of the most familiar artefacts pressed into jazz service. The washboard, a corrugated metal sheet framed in wood, served a rhythmic function when strummed by thimbled fingers. Remarkably, given its humble origin, it was sometimes billed as a featured instrument. The Washboard Rhythm Kings, the Washboard Rhythm Boys and Tinsley's Washboard Band were all names for the same band, which varied its billing almost from recording to recording. But whatever the brilliance of the players of 'legitimate' instruments, the belief was that the washboard possessed powers to give the band its unique identity, sufficient to lure listeners and dancers to their performances. One of the band's members even surrendered his given name in favour of his chosen instrument, to be known ever after as 'Washboard' Smith.

One of their many recordings was the transparently surreal 'All this World is Made of Glass'.

Queen of the washboardistes was **Beryl Bryden** (1920-1998), the big-voiced woman from Norwich who performed with a multitude of bands. It was during a visit to Australia that she secured a footnote in the record books, becoming the first person to be filmed playing the washboard under water.

In early bands the washboard would occasionally be found alongside another domestic fugitive, the washtub bass. The player plucked a string, one end of which was attached to the rim and the other to a broom handle opposite. By flexing the broom handle, the pitch could be varied slightly. Its musical properties were so limited that few, if any, practitioners achieved distinction. Its descendent was the tea-chest bass that spread like a rash during the skiffle boom of the 1950s, of which perhaps the less said the better.

Adrian Rollini (1904-1956) was sometimes called 'the multi-instrumentalists' multi-instrumentalist', a virtuoso performer on the piano (as a four-year-old he was giving Chopin recitals), bass and baritone saxophones, xylophone, vibraphone, cello and drums. He was also agile on the hot fountain pen. This was not a supercharged Waterman, favoured by authors of the racy prose of the 'jazz age', but a dinky little one-octave clarinet, invented by Adrian himself. It had its limitations, of course, but Rollini's genius was to overcome, even exploit, the limitations of any given instrument. Played by him, the ponderous bass saxophone with its low, low notes would positively twinkle. The smart bluffer should cite Rollini's happy brilliance, high and low, on 'A Mug of Ale', with Joe Venuti and his Blue Four, recorded in 1927.

If supporters of **Rahsaan Roland Kirk** (1936-1977) had

their way, there could be some jostling on the podium for the 'multi-instrumentalists' multi-instrumentalist' title, though Rollini's groupies could retort that Kirk's claim should be qualified as 'multi-weird-instrumentalist'. Manzello, stritch, trumpophone, slidesophone – all formed part of his armoury, together with tenor saxophone, clarinet, flute and piccolo, whistle and harmonica. For good measure he hung a toy xylophone round his neck and had, within arm's reach, a very large gong.

The manzello was a cousin of the soprano saxophone; the stritch was an alto, modified and made straight and long. The trumpophone was a hybrid, a trumpet with a saxophone mouthpiece; the slidesophone was a miniature trombone, again with a saxophone mouthpiece. Being festooned with these various instruments was remarkable enough, but more remarkable still was Kirk's ability to play tenor sax, manzello and stritch all at the same time. It was rumoured that he considered surgery to adapt his embouchure in order to add a baritone and hire himself out as a complete saxophone section.

Kirk was no mere novelty turn; like Rollini he was an inventive and masterly musician. He was just as inventive at naming his albums; here's a handful: *Does Your House Have Lions*, *Prepare Thyself to Deal with a Miracle*, *The Return of the 5,000 Lb Man* and *The Case of the 3 Sided Dream in Audio Color*. By the way, he also played the nose flute, an instrument that nobody was likely to ask to borrow.

Modern jazz came to Britain in the most romantic way. After the Second World War, a few Charlie Parker records arrived as ballast aboard a tramp steamer.

MORE BLUFFING ESSENTIALS

JAZZ DIVAS

When first you think of women in jazz during the formative years from the 1920s to the 1940s, only pianists and singers will readily come to mind. Some were outstanding. Lil Hardin (1898-1971) was a cornerstone of Louis Armstrong's Hot Five and Hot Seven. In fact, she married him. Mary Lou Williams (1910-1981) was an inventive player and brilliant arranger, notably for Andy Kirk and later for Dizzy Gillespie.

There were those who combined piano playing with singing, such as Cleo Brown (1909-1995) and Waller protégée Una Mae Carlisle (1915-1956), paving the way for the likes of Nina Simone (1933-2003) and Diana Krall (1964-). (You will controversially state that Simone, like Nat King Cole, was a better pianist than a singer.) Julia Lee (1902-1958) was a fine two-handed rocking pianist with a sly voice that she used to deliver cheekily smutty numbers such as 'I Didn't Like it the First Time'. The lyrics might refer to spinach but the meaning was concerned with something else entirely.

VALAIDA SNOW (1903-1956)

In the early days, women who played any instrument other than the piano, or sometimes the guitar, were so rare as to be deemed mere curiosities, irrespective of any talent they might have. One name that might briefly dazzle in a bluffing bout is Valaida Snow, a hot trumpet player much admired by Louis Armstrong and even more so by Earl Hines, who became her lover. She came to London in the mid-1930s and made some records; for a bonus point you could mention that the drummer was George Elrick, who became much more famous for being the presenter of *Housewives' Choice* on the BBC Light Programme.

ELLA FITZGERALD (1917-1996)

Thanks to 'Every Time We Say Goodbye', Ella Fitzgerald became perhaps the most widely known of all jazz singers. Her version of Cole Porter's sentimental dirge has become a firm favourite for funerals, ranked alongside Frank Sinatra's solipsistic anthem 'My Way' and Louis Armstrong's saccharine 'What a Wonderful World'. You will be on fairly safe ground when pointing out what a terrible irony it is that artists with such incredible jazz credentials should be best remembered for revealing that even they have feet of clay.

CONNEE BOSWELL (1907-1976)

Ella's earliest singing idol, Connee Boswell, was raised in New Orleans, the cradle of jazz, but not born there as many people think. And here's another irony: the woman

Ella admired so much was white, though to hear her you'd never know it. Connee had a deep, furry sound and an instinct for the rhythmic possibilities of whatever she sang. She acknowledged her own influences to be the Empress of the Blues, Bessie Smith (1894-1938), Louis Armstrong, Bing Crosby and Enrico Caruso. You will gain serious bluffing points for suggesting that her best recordings were made with her sisters, Martha and Vet. And the odd bonus point could come from a mention of the records she made with Crosby, which illustrate how they were obviously made for each other.

Funny how operatic tenors crop up as inspiration for jazz singers: Connee claimed Caruso, Crosby claimed John McCormack. There's no proof that Louis Armstrong swooned at the sound of the Italian tenor Beniamino Gigli, but there's no proof that he didn't either, so stir it in.

TEDDY GRACE (1905-1992)

Teddy Grace wasn't born in New Orleans either, but sang and sounded as though she should have been. For the record, she was actually born in Arcadia, which you know is the ancient Greek ideal of bucolic romanticism, except that this one was in Louisiana. She recorded with some of the greats, such as Charlie Shavers and Bud Freeman, as well as Bob Crosby's band. She literally sang her voice to destruction, losing it for good on a morale-boosting tour during the Second World War, and for the rest of her life was barely able to speak. Teddy is worth dealing into any bluffing bout, if only to bamboozle other bluffers who think she was a man. This gender confusion has parallels in literary bluffing. 'Oh, Evelyn Waugh, she's such a good writer, I admire her work immensely,' you might hear a badly briefed bluffer say as they're teetering on the edge of an elephant trap. Followed by 'And as for George Eliot, he has no equal', as they pitch headlong into it.

Some might say that the likes of Teddy, Connee, Julia and Una Mae are examples of the small change of jazz, but they are the bits of precious metal that's there to be found when you sort through the humbler coinage. You should always have a pocketful to scatter among your poorer bluffees.

And you must never forget to mention the two other female titans of jazz: Billie Holiday and Rosemary Clooney.

BILLIE HOLIDAY (1915-1959)

Holiday possessed one of those voices that could never be mistaken for anyone else's: intense, sad and filled with pain (genuinely felt). Some jazz purists might claim that she was a blues or 'pop' singer; but you won't stand for that. Answer dismissively that she actually transcended musical genres and that her singing style was unique and extraordinary.

ROSEMARY CLOONEY (1928-2002)

Clooney was no stranger to pain either, descending into a drink- and drug-fuelled depressive hell in her late 30s. Although this condition is actually obligatory for most jazz singers, she managed to haul herself out of the abyss and reinstated her reputation as an accomplished TV performer, actor and recording artist in the 1970s. Bluffers will need to know that she co-starred opposite Bing Crosby in *White Christmas* (1954) and that she was the much-loved aunt of George Clooney.

BRITISH JAZZ

Jazz – as you might well expect – took quite a while to catch on in the British Isles. In fact, there are still areas in the extreme Celtic fringes where it has so far failed to find a foothold. It was not simply because it was perceived as a predominantly black-inspired music; the Victorians had always had a high regard for minstrel shows and had welcomed to their shores the followers of the great Edwin Pearce Christy, founder of Christy's Minstrels. In the first place, it had to overcome so many rooted ideas and tribal customs: things like promenade concerts, the Bath Pump Room and the Palm Courts, the Band of the Grenadier Guards (not forgetting all those brass bands pumping and trilling away among the satanic mills of the North), the music hall, Gilbert and Sullivan, and *Hymns Ancient & Modern*.

In the second place, jazz turned out to be a bit low-class, a bit infra dig. The US practitioners who crossed the Atlantic proved to be a rough lot and drank heavily. Early British jazz was played by working-class Jewish lads from Whitechapel and beyond, who drank even more. Its prominent figures included a trumpeter from the East End called Nat Gonella, whose strong cockney accent made Georgia sound as if it was the next stop up the line from Hoxton.

There were those who tried to instil a bit of polish, like Henry 'The Boogeyman' Hall, a post-war bandleader who dressed and spoke immaculately, and a saxophonist called Buddy Featherstonhaugh (pronounced by some as Fanshawe or even Feastonhay). But in spite of their best endeavours, British polite society, particularly vicars and councillors, were horrified at the sounds that jazz made. They were particularly upset by the saxophone. A certain George Clutsam, who claimed to be an authority on the strength of having arranged an operetta called *Lilac Time*, cheered everybody up by predicting that it would never last; other well-known authorities insisted that it was ruining family life.

Around the late 1940s jazz slowly began to catch on, although it had a brief hiccup when one leading revivalist called George Webb was seen to play the piano with his braces showing. It was at this point, however, that the press discovered that one of the leading jazz trumpeters, Humphrey Lyttelton, had not only been a Guards officer but had been to Eton. It became the thing for the bowler-hatted brigade to swear allegiance to jazz on the strength of their identical qualifications. Many an ordinary jazz lover perked up when it was learned that no less a person than the Hon Gerald Lascelles, a cousin of the Queen, was an avid listener.

From now on jazz was eminently respectable and one of the arts, with a multitude of books written about it. There were setbacks from time to time, like the Beaulieu riots (instigated by Teddy Boys at the 1960 summer jazz festival of the same name) and a colourful cove called George Melly, but, on the whole, British jazz was decent and hard-working and not unlike the real thing.

Modern jazz came to Britain in the most romantic way. After the Second World War, a few Charlie Parker records arrived as ballast aboard a tramp steamer. Secretly meeting in cellars and West End flats where the curtains were permanently drawn, young London-based musicians like

♛

British jazz was decent and hard-working and not unlike the real thing.

Johnny Dankworth (who began as a clarinettist in Freddie Mirfield's Garbagemen, and later disavowed his chirpy-sounding forename to become plain, dignified John and, later still, Sir John), Ronnie Scott (only ever refer to him as 'Ronnie') and Tony Crombie listened to these records and underwent immediate religious conversion.

British musicians felt impelled to worship at the shrine of 52nd Street, New York, and in order to make the pilgrimage they signed on as unable seamen in Geraldo's Navy – Geraldo being an English bandleader, born Gerald Bright. As a lucrative sideline he placed jobbing musicians on cruise liners, and thus became the Fate Marable of the transatlantic crossings. On their return trips Johnny and Ronnie and the rest of the lads brought back 'Bop', as music and also as a way of life. So jazz, which had run out of rivers to go up, now put to sea – still travelling steerage, of course.

After the likes of Stan Tracey, Neil Ardley, Mike Garrick and Tony Coe had plugged away in near obscurity for decades, Britain benefited from several briefly fashionable jazz revivals in the 1980s and 1990s. It included two important big bands – the (mainly white) Loose Tubes, which spawned eccentric talents like the pianist Django Bates and the saxophonist Iain Ballamy, and the (mainly black) Jazz Warriors, which launched the saxophonist Courtney Pine and the singer Cleveland Watkiss. Purists may feel free to dismiss the recent output of all of them on the grounds that it has blundered around between hip hop, orchestral work and Scandinavian electronic music, but the bluffer – if not able to recall a personal favourite, such as Pine's *Destiny's Song + The Image Of Pursuance* – should tell anyone who is listening that some of these young players have a damn fine tone, and, what's more, most of them are sharp dressers – cool dudes who make the glossies from time to time.

BIG BANDS

In the early days, any group that augmented what was regarded as the classic line-up of cornet, clarinet, trombone, banjo and piano could be on the way to being defined as a big band. Some groups aspired to an even grander status. Thus pianist Teddy Wilson and six other musicians could be billed on a record label not as a mere band but an orchestra. But even Jelly Roll Morton was content to call his 1926 seven-piece band the Red Hot Peppers; it was only after two more years and adding three more players that he claimed to lead an orchestra. Bud Freeman settled for nine as being sufficient to call his band the Summa Cum Laude Orchestra.

But groups like these were biggish rather than big, and unlikely to be recognised as big bands in the same way that those of Fletcher Henderson, Jimmie Lunceford, Benny Goodman, Duke Ellington, Count Basie, Woody Herman and so on would be.

You might wonder aloud, rhetorically, how big a big band should be, going on to suggest an assembly of a dozen musicians, or perhaps a few more. That's what Andy Kirk believed and he went so far as to emphasise the numerical claim by billing his outfit as the Twelve Clouds of Joy, though he did cheat a bit by including a vocalist and a violinist. There could be no hard-and-fast rule as to the mix of instruments. From the 1930s onwards it generally worked out at four trumpets, three or four trombones, four or five saxophones, piano, bass, guitar and drums. However, some leaders found this a little restrictive and aspired to have still larger outfits. If, like Paul Whiteman, you crown yourself 'King of Jazz' and set about peddling 'Symphonic Syncopation', you might find it tiresome to settle for a band of fewer than 23, including violins and violas plus the occasional accordion and even a slide whistle.

Stan Kenton was prone to equate immensity with

intensity, mustering no fewer than 40 musicians for his 'Innovations' orchestra, performing grandly solemn-sounding works such as 'Ennui', 'Conflict', 'Trajectories', 'Incident in Jazz' and 'Artistry in...' (in this, that and the other). The orchestra of Eddie Sauter and Bill Finegan seldom fielded fewer than 20 players. Of course, bands like these were never intended to fulfil jazz bands' natural function of playing for dancing, though some promoters took a chance, booked them into ballrooms and lived to regret it for years afterwards. Musicians went hungry, but with their principles more or less intact. When one aggrieved couple shuffled up to the stand and asked a Sauter-Finegan trombonist, 'Why don't you play something we can dance to?' the reply was, 'Why don't you dance something we can play to?'

JAZZ TALKIN'

As with anything that has pretensions to being an art form, the enjoyment of the cognoscenti stems as much from talking about jazz as from actually listening to it. This extends to audiences who insist on applauding while it is being played. In jazz, the vocabulary is of less importance than one's general attitude. For instance, you must have a sense of period.

Take Duke Ellington as a sample subject. Refer to him as 'Duke' or 'The Duke'. You would be expected to know what was implied by succinct reference to his 1920s style (jungle noises over a bouncing tuba and banjo background); his 1930s style (jungle noises over a string bass and guitar background with optional timpani); the 1940s big-band stuff coloured by the genius of a short-lived bass player called Blanton; the rather more pretentious 1950s numbers with modernistic chords bolted on by an assistant pianist called Strayhorn (bluffer's tip: his nickname was 'Sweet Pea'); and the general decline of the 1960s. You don't have to agree with any of this; it's merely desirable to know what's being implied.

You need to understand that the demanding nature of jazz means that all jazzmen decline very quickly. After a brief period of being underrated, they find their distinctive tone, then in their 20s make the recordings by which they will always be known and become ambitious in their 30s, before turning 40 and taking the first steps down the road to oblivion.

As a large percentage of jazzmen tend to leave this world (the result of occupational or liquid excesses) at quite an early age, 40 is considered a very mature vintage. It is difficult to think of many prominent jazzmen who have not suffered decline. Some have simply remained permanently pickled, but generally most of them signal that they're getting out of touch by trying to do what they once did naturally and well in what they themselves consider to be a mature manner but which, to the discerning bluffer, simply shows a lack of spontaneity and even integrity.

♔

As a large percentage of jazzmen tend to leave this world at quite an early age, 40 is considered a very mature vintage.

Very few jazzmen mature well. One manifestation of loss of integrity is the big-band wish. Jazzmen who established a respectable reputation by playing with as few as two other people, having moved to success with groups varying from five to seven players, then get the urge to front a big band. Even this can be forgiven if the results remain funky enough, but many jazzmen, even quite modern ones, often get delusions of grandeur at this point and signal their imminent decline by the lavish employment of a string section. It is safe to say that all string sections have been disastrous in jazz. Not all of these indulgences are a complete disaster, though; arrangers now are more sensitive to the individual qualities of the soloist and write accordingly.

There are many approaches to adopt in talking about jazz, most of them based on various critical factions. A lot of early jazz talk came from a book called *Jazzmen* by Frederic Ramsey, which adopted a friendly sort of tone; for example:

> *He had a vibrato that was in keeping with his sweeping crescendos, and just a touch of blue quality. While he played he seemed oblivious of the smoke-filled room and the dancers. He sat hunched forward, his clarinet pointed towards the floor.*

Jazz enthusiasts still lap up that kind of thing.

Jazzmen, published in 1939, clearly belongs to the romantic age of jazz literature, indeed to the romantic age of jazz itself when it was important to build up colour and background rather than go into detailed discussions of the music. Later, an altogether different brand of critic was in command; for example:

> *The theoretician might claim that the blues scale is none other than that of the mode of D... Actually the blues*

scale has quite a different nature…The third and seventh degrees are lowered or not depending on how open or how disguised an allusion to the major scale is desired. Frequently, blue notes and unaltered examples of the same degree occur within a single phrase. Sometimes, the two are superimposed, and in such cases the blue note's being a kind of suspended appoggiatura is emphasised.

Of course, in the early days, no one guessed that the player hunched forward with his clarinet pointed toward the floor was actually suffering from a suspended appoggiatura. Many died of similar things before this was found out, whereas today they could be saved.

WHERE TO BE SEEN

A musician stops a passer-by in New York. 'How do you get to Carnegie Hall?' he asks. 'Practice,' comes the reply. When the Benny Goodman orchestra played there in 1938, it was the first time jazz and swing musicians had been permitted to stomp their stuff on the hallowed platform that was, for many years, the exclusive province of 'them classical cats'. During the concert, big bandleader Paul Whiteman's teeth were heard being soundly gnashed in a darkened room. He believed that he had a prior claim on Carnegie with his symphonic swing, but jazz purists dismissed him as lacking emotional depth.

In Los Angeles the barriers fell in 1944 when jazzmen stepped for the first time onto the stage of the Philharmonic Hall. The poster printer couldn't fit in 'Jazz at the Philharmonic', abbreviating it to 'Jazz at the Phil', and thus it remained for the next 40 years. Some good music was made, and so was some bad, encouraged by barbaric members of the audience screaming and whistling for more. Sadly, otherwise fine performers occasionally surrendered to this in a most unmusical manner, among them the tenor saxophonist Illinois Jacquet (with, you might wryly suggest, his fellow tenor players Alabama Trauzerz and Ohio Schirtanpanz) who demolished 'The Surrey With the Fringe on Top'. Mercifully, it was never released on record.

These big concerts were far removed from the original haunts of jazz – the brothels, speakeasies and cafés of New Orleans and Chicago, where the music was often an accompaniment to other more fleshly activities. Far removed were they, too, from their latter-day British counterparts.

Ronnie Scott's, for example, is a club with a worldwide reputation – a smart place, unblemished now by the carpet stains and cigarette burns that once lent it colour and atmosphere. Its earliest location was a Gerrard Street basement. Former patrons recall that it was often entered either by shinning down a rope or a firemen's pole. Not many are able to recall how they got out again.

One of the smallest, if not the smallest, venues ever recorded was situated in the front parlour of a modest house in Coventry. This was the Spirella, which also served as the fitting room for a corset maker (a plaque on the wall discreetly advertised the fact). Audiences of at least five or six crowded in to hear the resident band, trumpet player Deaf Rhubarb Blenkinsop (which attentive bluffers will recognise as one of the aforementioned great names in jazz history, albeit possibly apocryphal) and pianist Porridge Foot Pete. One session was taped, with the title *After Hours at the Spirella*. No copies are known to have survived.

DISCOGRAPHY/COLLECTING

Lots of jazz enthusiasts never go near live jazz. They listen to it entirely in recorded form. When they burble blithely about Armstrong's 1934 period, they are thinking entirely about the Armstrong sounds they happen to have on disc. Yet most jazz musicians were toiling away somewhere every night, and the few hours they spent in the recording studio were, to them, probably not representative of their best work.

It is partly the fault of jazz itself. Not being available in the shape of a score, the only evidence one can depend on is what the recording has preserved for posterity. Most jazz cannot be written down and disappears forever the moment it is played – or would if it were not for the timely presence of the occasional recording engineer. As most jazz talk is about jazz on record, the bluffer had better be well-briefed in this department.

These days, jazz buffs split into two strands:

1. Vinyl purists

2. CD converts.

(Note that jazz lovers rarely admit to downloading the stuff digitally; it's just not done – well, not yet).

Whichever side you support, make sure that you

argue your case with conviction and force. Vinyl purists will enthuse about retaining the 12-by-12 purity of Reid Miles's hip cover artwork on late-1950s Blue Note LPs; the indefinable warmth of a Prestige long player; the charming surface noise on those original Satchmo 78s. (You could hazard a bluff about analogue sound signals being unsuited to CD's 16-bit digital sampling process, but you might have to bail out if questioned further.)

The true jazz collector was, at one time, only interested in 78s. It was considered not to be the real thing unless it sounded as if it was being played several streets away with a rusty nail. However, as not many will enjoy the opportunity to own an original Gennett, Paramount or Okeh (early jazz record labels, the possession of which would be the equivalent of having a Shakespeare first folio), it has become acceptable to collect later reissues – so long as the original background noise is preserved.

The principal pastime with old recordings was to identify who was on them, so the dimness of the sound was simply an additional challenge. But there are still plenty of unsolved mysteries to promote enjoyable arguments. These generally revolve around who was playing, say, the cornet on the 1925 recording by the Mississippi Ramblers. Should someone hazard a guess that it was Jazzum Jenkins, you could pour scorn on this on account of the prominent use of the mute. Jenkins, as far as you know (which is not all that far really), never used a mute. A broken beer glass occasionally, but never a mute, which it clearly is here – unless he was standing behind a pillar. And so it goes on.

The collector is particularly intrigued by alternative takes. As most early jazzmen on most early sessions were inclined to be playing under the influence of alcohol or something else of a mind-altering nature, the takes were inclined to be many in number. It is a well-known fact, even in today's highly professional recording circles, that having tried seven or eight alternative versions of a given piece, the producer always decides that the first take was the best anyway, and this is generally the one issued. But occasionally someone misunderstands the producer's scrawl and types out 'Take 3' instead. This becomes an everlasting source of discographical interest.

In the expansive LP era it became the thing to reissue all the alternative takes side by side so that the collector could hear what went wrong. You can now hear for yourself how things got progressively worse as the alcohol took effect and the trombonist's lips fell apart. Some scrupulous editors have dug around and put out every scrap of discarded tape. It is an ineffable delight to the earnest collector to hear Charlie Parker bitterly complaining that he is having reed trouble.

Meanwhile, CD converts will praise the crisp sound quality and longer uninterrupted playing time– the fact that Coltrane's *Live In Seattle* sees him improvise continuously for over an hour (didn't he ever need to visit the Gents?) or that we can now hear Art Tatum's piano playing without all the extraneous recording noises (even if most of them were made by Tatum himself). CD jazz fans will also point out that thousands of rare-as-hen's-teeth recordings are now getting thrown out on CD since it's quite cheap for record companies to manufacture them – much cheaper, of course, than commissioning a new recording.

For the collector, two pieces of harmless discographical pleasure remain. One stems from the fact that although the durations of tracks are often printed on labels and/or sleeves, they are always wrong – not by a minute or any explainable misprint but by some arbitrary amount. When all other conversation has lapsed, you can always take out your stopwatch and run a book on who can guess the nearest correct answer. The other is the habit indulged in by some compilers of reissues, of splicing together solos from different takes of the same tune. The object of the game in this instance is to try to spot the joins in what purports to be one continuous performance. It's the musical equivalent of wig-spotting.

It's been commonly asserted over the years, mostly by people who have never tried to listen to it, that Miles Davis's *Bitches Brew* is one of the most essential albums ever recorded.

NEED-TO-KNOW ALBUMS

This is the age of the list, the Top This, That and The Other, so it may be wise for the bluffer to avoid venturing abroad without a list of his or her own. Other bluffers will certainly have theirs. But which list should be at your fingertips? Coming back like a song, year in, year out, is the inventory of so-called top albums, though what function such a list might serve, when opinions are entirely subjective, is open to question. Never mind. When lists are flying like shuttlecocks, you might as well bat your own over the net. Other bluffers might disagree with your nominations, but nobody can ever say you're wrong. That's the beauty of bluffing. Try these, in no particular order.

BITCHES BREW
MILES DAVIS (1969/70)

It's been commonly asserted over the years, mostly by people who have never tried to listen to it, that this is one of the most essential albums ever recorded, both electric and eclectic. It's that all right, with lots of bubbling, toiling, troubling and cackling as Miles perches atop a craggy rock, screeching away for all he's worth. Everybody involved seems hell-bent, literally, on immersing any morsels of the jazz tradition in a cauldron of slugs and snails and puppy dogs' tails. Bluffers might adopt an air of gravitas and say: 'I've always felt it sounds like Stockhausen meeting Boulez, with neither relishing the encounter.' Essential? It might be useful to have as a means of persuading guests who have outstayed their welcome to go – much more effective than patting cushions or getting the Hoover out.

This is the sort of album you'd be inclined to play to people who might be about to leave but whom you'd prefer to stay.

THE INCREDIBLE JAZZ GUITAR OF WES MONTGOMERY (1960)

This is the sort of album you'd be inclined to play to people who might be about to leave but whom you'd prefer to stay. One list in which it crops up suggests that we 'forget Django Reinhardt'. Don't be swayed by the view of an obvious fathead. On the evidence of these performances Wes Montgomery certainly hasn't forgotten Django, nor has he forgotten Charlie Christian. He's picked up the baton handed on by them, and he hears them even as he fashions his own brilliant music.

SONGS FOR SWINGIN' LOVERS
FRANK SINATRA (1955)

Frank Sinatra and Nelson Riddle could take a good deal of credit for realising the form of the so-called 'concept' album – songs and sounds that can stand on their individual merits but, taken together, make for a coherent whole. *Songs for Young Lovers* and *Swing Easy!* were their first essays in the genre, dating from 1953, and each of those should nudge their way into any listing of top albums, but each would have to bow to *Swingin' Lovers* for prime placing. Sinatra is the ultimate big-band singer and Riddle provides the ultimate big band for him to prove it, with economical but telling trumpet solos from Harry 'Sweets' Edison. Like Sinatra, Riddle had an impeccable swing-band pedigree, including playing trombone with Tommy Dorsey, Sinatra's former boss.

TIME OUT
THE DAVE BRUBECK QUARTET (1959)

It might have bewildered the critics and a good many of Brubeck's core audience at first, but this became one of the best-selling jazz albums ever. The title derives from the fact that the music deviates from orthodox jazz time signatures and renders numbers based on pulses of five or seven beats to a bar. *Take Five* became a huge commercial success in its own right. You might also offer the view that the real heroes of these excursions into alien time signatures are bass player Eugene Wright and, even more so, the genius drummer Joe Morello who makes sure that, no matter how many beats there are to a bar, the whole thing still swings.

APRIL IN PARIS
COUNT BASIE (1957)

Insist that this is one of the best bands that Basie ever had, with a wonderfully loose, splashy rhythm section underpinned by Sonny Payne's drums. The title track, Vernon Duke's classic tune, became so popular that it was issued on a 12-inch 78rpm disc. 'One more time,' calls Basie. There's a crisp roll on the drums and the band repeats the coda with added high notes from the trumpets. 'Let's try it one more once,' urges Basie. Another drum roll, another coda, with trumpets flying higher yet. It still thrills. There were some fine soloists in this band: trumpet players Joe Newman and the more boppish Thad Jones; the two Franks on tenors, Foster and Wess; and the Count himself on piano.

ELLINGTON AT NEWPORT
DUKE ELLINGTON (1956)

This marked something of a comeback for the Duke. When he and the band took the stand at the 1956 Newport Jazz Festival, the audience was respectfully pleased at the appearance of a distinguished member of the jazz nobility. By the time the last notes of 'Diminuendo In Blue and Crescendo in Blue' had been sounded, that same audience was a frenzied, near-hysterical mob close to riot. The culprit was tenor player Paul Gonsalves who took 27 hot, rocking choruses. Bluffers might advance the view that this sort of showmanship is all very well if you're there, but on record it does tend to pale after a couple of playings. Say that better music was made that day – 'Blues to be There', for instance.

SAXOPHONE COLOSSUS
SONNY ROLLINS (1956)

Nobody could claim that Rollins made a handsome sound on the tenor saxophone. If it weren't for his sizzling invention and nimble articulation, his playing could be confused with the sort of noises a struggling beginner might come up with. 'Blue 7' runs at over 11 minutes. Rollins's imagination never flags, and pianist Tommy Flanagan is with him every step of the way, as are bass player Doug Watkins and drummer Max Roach, who solos by deploying sticks on every bit of his kit, including bits you're not supposed to hit. 'St Thomas' is a calypso-tinged homage to the Virgin Islands – a chirpy little theme, morsels of which lodge in the memory. Bluffers might whistle bits to impress.

FOCUS
STAN GETZ (1961)

The seeds of this album were sown in the 1940s, when Stan Getz and Eddie Sauter were on Benny Goodman's payroll – Getz among the saxophones, Sauter writing some of the arrangements. Getz claimed this to be his personal favourite of all his recordings. By any standards, say that it's music making of the highest order, a combination of tightly scored orchestral themes by Sauter, over and through which Getz improvises, like threads in a tapestry. Nothing was written for Getz to play, though he was given a sketch of each piece for guidance. There's no rhythm section but Getz makes it swing. You can say confidently that it doesn't conform to the generally accepted definition of jazz, but jazz is indisputably in this music. All you have to do is listen.

LOUIS ARMSTRONG PLAYS WC HANDY (1954)

It stands to reason that any self-respecting bluffer, even a beginner, will have made the acquaintance of the classic recordings of Armstrong's Hot Five and Hot Seven. Reissues have emerged over the years on a variety of labels. But apart from a couple of concert recordings, this might be claimed as Louis's first album proper. It's a dazzling band, the same as could be seen in *High Society*, with one exception: in the film the clarinet is played by Edmond Hall; on the album it's Barney Bigard. (Many bluffer's points awarded for throwing this in.) Thanks to a spot of multi-tracking trickery, on 'Atlanta Blues' Louis sings to his own trumpet obbligato and then scats along with himself. Louis times three, for the price of one.

UNDER MILK WOOD
STAN TRACEY (1965)

As resident pianist at Ronnie Scott's for many years, Stan Tracey took a certain grim pleasure in pointing out to visiting piano players that the instrument installed in the 'old place' was less than perfect. 'From 'ere to 'ere, they don't work,' he'd say, indicating the keyboard. His own piano playing, with hints of Thelonius Monk, was a revelation to visiting US musicians. 'Does anybody here know how good he is?' was often asked by an open-mouthed Yank. Stan wrote the suite *Under Milk Wood*, inspired by Dylan Thomas's radio play, declaring himself 'quite knocked out' with it. Tracey and tenor player Bobby Wellins, together with Jeff Clyne on bass and Jackie Dougan on drums, reflect its atmosphere brilliantly. (Here's a 'by-the-way' for bluffers: the original broadcast of the play was narrated by Richard Burton.)

There's no point in pretending that you know everything about jazz – nobody does – but if you've got this far and you've absorbed at least a modicum of the information and advice contained within these pages, then you will almost certainly know more than 99% of the rest of the human race about what jazz is, where it comes from and who plays it. What you now do with this information is up to you, but here's a suggestion: be confident about your newfound knowledge, see how far it takes you but, above all, have fun using it. After all, you are now a bona fide expert in the art of bluffing about the world's hippest, heppest, downright hottest musical art form.

Think you're ready to shine with your knowledge of jazz? Test it first with our quiz at bluffers.com.

GLOSSARY

Acid jazz Marketing man's term (circa 1990) for a kind of pop music that occasionally involved saxophones.

Big-band jazz Purist's term of abuse for: a) any group containing more than seven players; b) any group that has two or more saxophones in it. Those in favour of the whole idea refer to it as 'the bread'.

Cat A fashionable jazz-loving gentleman (*see* 'Man'). Also the suffix of 'hepcat', a seriously fashionable jazz-loving gentleman.

Commercial Term of abuse for jazz that is likely to appeal to the general public, a body of people much despised by the jazz fraternity.

Corn Term of abuse for jazz that is likely to appeal to the general public, who are frequently referred to by the jazz fraternity as 'cornflakes'.

Creole A term of respectability, implying some useful (especially French) interbreeding and lighter shades of black. Used as an elevating title by bands such as the Creole Jazz Band.

Dixieland A source of total confusion since Dixieland, as a geographical term, means the southern US states with banjos strumming and all that jazz; but as a generic term (because of the Original Dixieland Jazz Band) is generally applied to white groups playing in a frivolous style and wearing bowler hats and star-spangled waistcoats.

Fake book Book that all jazz musicians must own containing the melody and chords of many standards and jazz themes – *The Advanced Bluffer's Guide to Jazz,* if you will.

Funky smelly Has occasionally been linked with the word 'butt', meaning a bottom. Fortunately it has changed its meaning somewhat to imply earthiness, bluesiness, gospelarity, Africanality, etc.

Gone Term used, in the peculiarly boomerang manner of much jazz terminology, to imply a definite state of being here and going places.

Growl Noise made by an underpaid trombonist.

Hep Also hip. The state of being in the know. Refer to a jazz club or festival as a hip operation, changing the record as a hip replacement, and so on.

Hot The most glowing tribute you can pay to traditional jazz. A mind-singeing way of playing. Known as 'warm' when applied to mainstream jazz and 'cool' when applied to modern.

Jam When everyone plays together with no clear idea of where they are going or even what they are playing, or who with. Chiefly amusing to those who are doing it but occasionally results, by chance, in something coherent and exciting.

Jive In the past (1930s), a hectic type of dancing also known as jitterbugging in the pre-rock world. Now more usually applied to jazz talk. A telling phrase in any bluffer's vocabulary, said in tones of deep disbelief, is: 'Don't give me that jive, man!'

Latin jazz Jazz improvisation played over bossa-nova or Afro-Cuban rhythms. Or, perhaps, a first-century prototype of bebop played by Ovid.

Man Initially used as a means of address by African-American jazz musicians who were tired of being called 'boy' by white racists. Now used by many as a random punctuation point in a sentence.

Modal Strange Indo-Arabic-sounding scales, often used by modern jazzers, that aren't diatonic major, minor or blues scales. If a solo starts sounding odd, just describe it as 'modal'.

Mouldy fig Sort of person who likes or plays trad.

Name band Friendly sort of outfit ready to do anything to please the public, the title deriving from the phrase: 'You name it, we'll play it'.

Revivalist Polite term for the old white folks in stripy blazers and straw boaters who play trad and Dixieland. *See* also 'Mouldy fig'.

Rhythm Element in jazz that either you 'got' or didn't. Disliked by English vicars and old spinsters in the early days as it tended to rattle the cake stands.

Rhythm changes Chord changes to the old Gershwin song 'I Got Rhythm', which provided the basis for a lot of bebop. Usually played at such a rhythm as to be unrecognisable.

Riff A phrase generally repeated ad nauseam by sections of a big band. Deriving from 'The Riff Song', a chorus repeated ad nauseam in *The Desert Song*.

Rock, rocking Originally another rude word connected with sexual activity, but latterly attached to jazz in the purely descriptive sense of a band that is really swinging, in the groove, smokin', stompin', or whatever you like, really.

Scat A method of getting over a temporary aberration concerning the words of any song.

Scratch band Local line-up hastily assembled to accompany a famous touring musician – 'scratch' because the band spend most of their time scratching their heads while trying to read unfamiliar arrangements.

Shuffle A dance step originated by reluctant males at endlessly dreary dinner-dances.

Smooth jazz Name given to the bland soul and funk instrumentals which comprise the playlist of most 'jazz' radio stations and act as a cure for insomnia. No self-respecting bluffer should dignify this as 'jazz'.

Standards Broadway show tunes and US pop songs of the 1920s, 1930s and 1940s that have become requisite material for jazz musicians. The implication is that post-war pop isn't as good, or that 'standards' are declining.

Third stream Term coined by the composer Gunther Schuller in the 1950s to mean a fusion of jazz and classical music. About as meaningful as the 'third way' coined 40 years later by Tony Blair.

Trad a) a piece of music that can freely be used because nobody knows who wrote it and it costs nothing; b) jazz played by mouldy figs.

Wail, wailing Contrary to what one might think, a complimentary term for one who is playing with considerable savoir faire and soul.

BLUFFING NOTES

Bluffing Notes

Bluffing Notes

Bluffing Notes

Bluffing Notes

Bluffing Notes

....
....
....
....
....
....
....
....
....
....
....
....
....
....
....
....
....
....
....
....
....
....
....
....
....
....
....

Bluffing Notes

Bluffing Notes

Bluffing Notes

Bluffing Notes

....
....
....
....
....
....
....
....
....
....
....
....
....
....
....
....
....
....
....
....
....
....
....
....
....
....
....

Bluffing Notes

Bluffing Notes

Bluffing Notes

Bluffing Notes

Bluffing Notes